THIS IS NOT

THE IVY LEAGUE

AMERICAN LIVES

Series editor: Tobias Wolff

THIS IS

NOT THE

IVY LEAGUE

{A MEMOIR}

Mary Clearman Blew

UNIVERSITY OF NEBRASKA PRESS ∾ LINCOLN AND LONDON

Acknowledgments for the use
    of previously published
material appear on page vii,
        which constitutes an extension
of the copyright page.

Publication of this volume
    was made possible in part
by the generous support
    of the H. Lee and Carol
Gendler Charitable Fund.

Library of Congress Cataloging-
    in-Publication Data
Blew, Mary Clearman, 1939–
    This is not the Ivy League: a
memoir / Mary Clearman Blew.
        p. cm. — (American lives)
ISBN 978-0-8032-3011-8
    (cloth: alkaline paper)
1. Blew, Mary Clearman, 1939–
    —Family. 2. Montana—
Biography. I. Title.
    PS3552.L46Z46 2011
813'.54—dc22
        [B]   2011004073

Set in Janson by Bob Reitz.
    Designed by Nathan Putens.

For Joy Passanante and Gary Williams
With thanks for these years of friendship

ACKNOWLEDGMENTS

The prologue originally appeared in Jennifer Sinor and Rona Kaufman, eds., *Placing the Academy* (Logan: Utah State University Press, 2007).

Chapter 1 originally appeared in Zachary Michael Jack, ed., *Black Earth and Ivory Tower* (Columbia: University of South Carolina Press, 2005). Reprinted with permission.

A different version of chapter 2 originally appeared in *The Georgia Review* (Summer 2011).

Chapter 3 originally appeared in Mary Clearman Blew, *All But the Waltz* (1991; repr., Norman: University of Oklahoma Press, 2001). © 1991 by Mary Clearman Blew. Reprinted with permission.

Chapter 4 is reprinted from *Prairie Schooner* 84, no. 2 (Summer 2010) by permission of the University of Nebraska Press. © 2010 by the University of Nebraska Press.

Chapter 6 originally appeared in Caroline Patterson, ed., *Montana Women Writers: A Geography of the Heart* (Helena MT: Farcountry Press, 2008).

Chapter 7 originally appeared in *The Gettysburg Review* 19, no. 4 (Winter 2006). Reprinted with permission.

Chapter 8 originally appeared in *Shenandoah* 50, no. 1 (Spring/ Summer 2009).

The epilogue originally appeared in *Copper Nickel* 10 (2008).

Prologue

Landscape. What one can see in a single view. Drive west toward Seattle at seventy or eighty miles an hour on Interstate 90, and landscape will be a rolling gray blur of sagebrush through the insulation of the car window, the dammed and degraded Columbia River a brief glimpse of silver, a few raw towns bypassed, and then two double-lane highways unfurling upward through inky fringes of evergreens that hide the giant patches where timber is being harvested on the Cascade Range.

Never mind the timber. From the warmth of the car, what is visible through a veil of rain on the windshield is the endless interstate and the busy, increasing traffic that nips in and out as double lanes become triple lanes for the descent down the west side of the Cascades, triple lanes and access lanes and underpasses and loops and whorls buzzing with traffic, past towns with names that used to have meanings, Snoqualmie, Issaquah, only a blur, until finally there's the skyline of Bellevue on the east shore of Lake Washington, great glass and steel towers completely surrounded by residential developments and featureless strips and malls and parking garages and apartment complexes beyond complexes beyond complexes, all looped and overlooped by freeways meeting freeways, freeways passing over and under freeways, serpentine and circumferencing freeways.

Landscape. The single view. Pull over the automobile in one of those trouble lanes, step outside that upholstered cocoon with the string quartet emanating from the speakers and the smell of coffee from the vacuum cup, and landscape becomes a stench of heated tires and exhaust and a cacophony of hurtling, shrieking metal, tons of metal, seven or eight lanes of shrieking, speeding metal like a crazed herd bent only on speed, speed. What is their destination, what is contained in those single human heads so briefly visible through the flash of glass, only they know. Learning the purpose in what looks like chaos is not the task at hand. The task at hand is learning whether there is a way through the labyrinth of freeways on foot. Whether it is possible to walk along what looked from the automobile like a low-lying streak of silver, what now turns out to be a line of buckled and dented metal rails fixed to short posts, whether it is possible to walk here without being struck from behind by one of those crazed, speeding hunks of metal and turned into a sodden pulp.

Surely there is a way to cross over. Coyotes and raccoons, survivors to the last, sniff out trails along forgotten creek beds and ravines. They sneak through brush and Scotch broom, dart openly where they must, turn up in backyards to gobble the food left out for a cat. But can a young woman, if her life depends upon it, cross the freeway and reach one of those apartment complexes, clearly visible on the other side of the seven or eight lanes of hurtling metal?

IN ONE OF THOSE anonymous apartment complexes within a labyrinth of freeways in Bellevue, Washington, during the winter of 1969 there lived a young woman who lay awake at night and listened to the roar of traffic that ebbed around three in the morning but never completely died away. She had spent the past five years in a graduate literature program at the University of Missouri in Columbia, but now that she had successfully defended her dissertation, she had nothing to do and nowhere to go. She and her husband had moved to the Pacific Northwest because Seattle was their dream city, and she had expected to find a college or university teaching job, but there were no jobs, or at least none she could find in Seattle or its sprawling suburbs. During the days, after her husband had left for the junior high school where he taught, and while her children attended their elementary school, she obsessively cleaned the apartment and tried to read or sew, and at night she lay awake listening to the buzz of the freeways and wondering where her life had gone wrong.

In later years she would wonder why she hadn't done more to help herself. It was true she was trapped without transportation behind the loops and whorls of the buzzing freeways, but it was also true that a shuttle bus traveled daily from one of the Bellevue motels to downtown Seattle, and surely she could have learned the schedule and found a way on foot through the freeways to the motel. Perhaps another woman would have made the effort, enjoyed the city, wandered along the piers in the heady salt breezes off Elliot Bay, browsed in the shops, bought a few exotic vegetables or spices in the open-air market. But she didn't. The city wasn't what she wanted; what she wanted was a job. Without a job she had nothing to do, nothing that mattered, and yet she felt exhausted, dragged down by some strange buzzing force that she didn't understand, weighted by the effort of getting through another day of small tasks.

Everyone who knew her was baffled by her unhappiness. Here she was, living in a comfortable apartment with a faithful, hard-working husband and two beautiful children. If she thought she had to have a job, she could find one right there in Bellevue. Secretarial jobs, clerking jobs—did she think she was too good for a secretarial job? What gave her that idea? It was 1969, after all, and the women's magazines were filled with dire warnings for women who tried to pursue careers—she was being self-centered, selfish—and our young woman didn't disagree, she was willing to accept whatever label anyone pasted on her, but she wasn't willing to accept the dead end she'd found herself in. Why were there no college or university teaching jobs in literature, when there had always been jobs, when she had been told there always would be jobs? Was it some flaw in herself, some inadequacy she had never forced herself to face?

(It was 1969. The Modern Language Association hadn't started publishing its job listings yet, there were no articles about the sudden surplus of young PhDs in the humanities, hundreds of young PhDs in the humanities, hundreds more being churned out by the graduate schools in the next year and the next, and hardly any jobs. It would take some time before the young PhDs would realize they were all in the same boat. In 1969 our young woman supposed that she was the only one who couldn't find a job, and her sense of failure ate away at her.)

What are we to make of this young woman, looking back at her after so many years? That she was naïve—well, to say the least! Tiresomely naïve, and tiresomely self-absorbed, as though she had no idea how narrow her view of the world was, how scant her experience. She did possess a kind of dumb determination. Endurance was probably her strongest point. She hung on for the long haul, yes she did.

She and her husband had married in a seethe of teenage lust to the lyrics of popular music and almost immediately were disappointed to discover that they were married to each other and not to their ideas of each other. But they were making the best of it. They had their children to consider, after all. They both came from families where marriage was for life. Also, they both were afraid of what life might do to them without the other as a prop. So they made the best of it. They did collect grievances like troll's gold, however, counting coins of resentment in secret and letting them pile up.

What became of the young woman? Did she sit in that Bellevue apartment, weeping and spinning her troll's gold out of flammable straw, until her mind blurred into the inexorable buzz of freeway traffic? Was she finally crushed into some semblance of a teacher's wife by the weight of all that pavement? Lost within those miles of curving triple and quadruple lanes and loops and interstices, the roaring overpasses and echoing underpasses and the dizzy busy cloverleafs, as tangled and snarled and knotted as though they had become, not just the labyrinth, but the very thread of Ariadne, spun into a concrete monster?

No. She didn't. What she did was to pore over the classifieds in the *Seattle Times* as the winter passed and the summer dragged into July, until one day she came upon an advertisement for what seemed to her the last academic job in the world. An assistant professor of English was wanted at Northern Montana College in Havre, Montana. *Call Dr. George Craig, Chairman*, the ad read, and listed a phone number.

She dialed. Listened to a faraway ring.

"Northern Montana College," said a throaty voice from six hundred miles away.

"Dr. George Craig, please?"

"I don't think he's in the building. Wait a minute—I think I just saw him walk by."

The young woman could hear running footsteps and the voice calling, "Dr. Craig! Dr. Craig! You've got a phone call!" She was trying to visualize what kind of college she had reached when the phone was picked up again and a man said, cautiously, "Hello?"

"My name is Mary Clearman," she began, "and I saw your ad in the *Seattle Times*—"

"Do you have a doctorate?" he interrupted.

"Well, yes, I defended last December." She was going to continue, to explain her teaching experience, the subject of her dissertation (*Aspects of Juvenal in Ben Jonson's Comical Satires*), her published article in the *Keats-Shelley Journal*, the other journals where she had submitted articles, the letters of recommendation that she could have sent to him, but Dr. Craig gave her no time.

"Would you like to come for an interview?"

"Well—*yes*," she said, after a startled instant.

"You do have your doctorate."

"Yes."

"We'll send you an airline ticket."

LANDSCAPE. What one can see in a single view. It's only her second time in flight, and, twisting in her cramped seat to look down at the miniaturized interstate threading its way through the Cascade Range, she marvels at the way her perspective has been so abruptly altered. From the lofty altitude of thirty thousand feet she can see the square patches of managed timber reduced to a quilt in varying greens, and also the untouched and hollowed peaks that once belched and rumbled fire and lava in a forgotten eon but now hold lakes like tiny mirrors that reflect even tinier clouds and passing shadows until they, too, are lost from her view. The mountains roll back, the gray prairie stretches to the Rockies and the prairie beyond the Rockies that she never expected to be returning to. The flight from Seattle has taken less than two hours.

On the airport tarmac in Great Falls, Montana, the wind hits her in the face and rips off her false eyelashes, which she snatches out of thin gritty air as they fly by, to the momentary astonishment of the passenger walking behind her. Inside the terminal she darts into the women's room to repair her face and sees—what. A face she's never had confidence in, hence the ridiculous false eyelashes and the hair stiffened by spray, and now she must take this inadequate face to meet the impatient Dr. George Craig, whose abrupt invitation for an interview she and her husband have puzzled over.

She squares her shoulders and forces herself to walk out of the shelter of the women's room and into the dusty white light where a few rows of cracked plastic seats and a vending machine are the only amenities in this country terminal, and a handful of passengers are still waiting for their luggage, and a short man with a graying crew cut has approached a very fat young woman in sandals and a faded sundress:

"Are you Dr. Clearman?"

The fat woman shakes her head, suspicion crossing her face as though he's made an indecent suggestion, and turns her back, and now there's nothing for our young woman but to get a grip, step up, and admit, "I'm Dr. Clearman."

He turns, stares at her. In her high heels she's a head taller than he is. Forever after she wonders if he would rather she had been the woman in the sundress and sandals.

IT TAKES ABOUT TWO hours to drive from the airport through Great Falls and north on Highway 87 to Havre (population something less than ten thousand), which lies along the Milk River, thirty miles short of the Canadian border. Rainfall up here on the high prairie averages about eleven inches a year, and the hot wind is constant, burning off what moisture there is and draining the color out of the landscape. Newcomers, expecting the spectacular Montana of the mountains to the south and west, are likely to be stunned, then appalled, at the endless shades of gray. Sagebrush on low hills and cutbanks, shadows of clouds, emptiness between earth and sky. *People really live out here?*

Yes, but not very many. Montana, with over 145,000 square miles making it the fourth-largest state in the United States, has a population of about eight hundred thousand, of which fewer than a hundred thousand live along that 250-mile northern stretch between Glasgow and Shelby known as the Highline, where James J. Hill built his railroad during the heyday of the homestead movement in 1910 in hopes of transforming the desert into a cornucopia of 320-acre family farms. Rain will follow the plow, he promised the homesteaders, but of course it didn't, and the farms failed during the drought of the 1920s and the depression of the 1930s.

With passing years, dryland farming techniques and hybrid seeds have turned the prairie into a cornucopia of wheat, but not in the way Hill imagined. Today the farms are vast, and one man with monster machinery representing a capital investment of hundreds of thousands of dollars can cultivate and harvest the acreage once tilled by twenty men. As the population grows sparser, it grows grayer. The young leave to find work, while the old watch satellite television and drive miles on paved single-lane highways to do their shopping. They worry about the weather and curse the federal government, but when some well-meaning researcher suggests, *Why not turn this prairie back into grazing land for buffalo and antelope? Who lives out here, anyway?* they answer in a thin but sturdy chorus: *We do!*

But we're trying to cover too much local history here, and also we're getting ahead of our story. In late July of 1969, the impervious clouds float high above their shadows, the sun beats down, and hawks keep watch from the crossbars of power poles for anything that moves. It may be hard for many to imagine living in such a country, slowed to the pace of a pulse through the heat and the wheat, but our young woman doesn't have to imagine. She knows the scent of sunbaked seeds and the pungency of sagebrush, the scratch of wheatheads on her arms and legs, she knows how sweat feels when it trickles through her hair and how barbed wire sounds when it sings in the wind. The sun weighs down upon her, drags her toward the drowsy earth where the stones and bones are buried. She'll be buried here if she isn't careful. She knows something about a kind of isolation that is different from what she knew in Bellevue: the isolation of distance and weather and the isolation of minds.

Yes, she knows a little of what she's getting into as the car with the State of Montana license plates driven by Dr. George Craig creeps north through ripening wheatfields riven by sage-choked coulees. She can see that Dr. George Craig knows this highway well, but he keeps glancing at her, trying to gauge her reactions.

The truth is, news of the PhD glut hasn't reached northern Montana. Dr. George Craig needs to hire an assistant professor with a PhD if his college is going to keep its accreditation; he needs to hire a PhD so badly that, well, he'd probably not commit murder for one, but short of that. Is there any possibility at all that this stiff young woman from Seattle in her dark green linen dress and her teased hair and her false eyelashes would come to this place to live?

At last he ventures, "Is this your first visit to Montana?"

"Oh, no," she says, "I was born and raised here," and to her astonishment, he lets out his breath in relief.

So you know what you're getting into.

As they near Havre, George Craig turns off State 87 onto the old highway, which angles past the wheatfields to meet the welcome green of a few willows and box elder trees and the windswept roofs of houses with small watered lawns. The young woman is trying to mesh what she sees with the only other time she visited Havre, with her father when she was in her teens and they were chasing an auctioneer who had stolen a milk cow. Also, the story her grandmother used to tell, about driving up to Havre from the homestead with a team and wagon to meet the train from the east, and camping overnight on the prairie on the way up and the way back. What a growing-up she's had, if George Craig only knew. He'll never know, if it's up to her. Not that she's ashamed of her background, exactly, but it seems too complicated to explain, on the one hand, and irrelevant on the other. She's a scholar, after all, she's spent years learning Latin and reading the classics, so what do stolen milk cows have to do with her?

She'll live long enough to consider the answer to that question, to understand that her scholarship grew from her fear of suffocation, of being buried alive under that blinding sun. Also, to her surprise, she'll live to see Montana transformed from nowhere to somewhere glamorous (though never the Highline, it will never be glamorous, not the shortgrass prairie up here on the northern brow of the world where the wind blows constantly, and the sun beats down, and the temperature rises to over 110 degrees in the summer and drops to minus 45 degrees in the winter). But the glamorization of Montana and the West lies far in the future. Right now George Craig is driving past the streets of modest houses where the wind has bowed the trees and scoured paint off sidings, and he is stopping on a bluff overlooking the Milk River with the town of Havre curled around it. Perched on the brow of the bluff, interrupting endless dusty blue sky, is the campus of Northern Montana College.

He parks in front of one of the buildings. Two long brick wings support a squat tower that will hold the next eighteen years of her life.

"This is Cowan Hall."

PLACE IS WHERE WE imagine ourselves to be. Juvenal's Rome of the second century, for example. *Who but the wealthy get sleep in Rome?* The mobs, the noise, the surging crowds, the dense mass of people—why did the Montana girl ever choose to walk those dangerous streets in the footsteps of the old satirist? Or the equally congested streets of Ben Jonson's seventeenth-century London—what was she looking for? Yes, it's true in part that she was fleeing the silence of the high plains, it's true in part that she was trying to reinvent herself in a milieu as far removed as she could find from the place she was born, or from what she was intended to be. Years later her gorge still rises when she thinks about the dearth of expectations for her, the easy way the ranch girl's dreams were dismissed.

But to settle for the suffocation theory is to overlook a single truth about the woman the Montana girl was becoming: she loved the work of scholarship. Loved it. Loved her painstaking translations from the Latin, loved the careful juxtaposition of texts, loved the language, loved the complex tracery of ideas and images that the old satirist passed on from Rome to London. Most of all she loved the timelessness of absorbing herself in her work, the out-of-body experience of dissolving library walls and fading street sounds, the sensation of one mind touching another over centuries through words. Was she naïve in her love, as she was naïve in so many other ways? Unaware of how ridiculous she looked, with the dust of carrels and seldom-opened texts filtering down on her stiff-sprayed hair, her makeup? Yes, call her naïve, call her ridiculous, but still admit that single truth: she loved her scholarship.

And if she returns to Montana? In that first moment on the steps of Cowan Hall, she has a dim inkling of the battles she will have to fight if she returns, but how fierce the battles, how stiff the price she'll pay, she cannot possibly imagine. Who could imagine an assistant professorship costing her her scholarly work? Or her marriage? Who could have imagined Northern Montana College?

It's as though a tribe of gypsies camped here one night and decided to start a college, remarked one of her colleagues, years later, but it wasn't gypsies, it was sodbusters who founded Northern in the 1930s, in the depths of a depression that sent every starved and windblown community scrambling for whatever public institutions might provide a payroll. A college, why not. Havre was three hundred miles over bad roads from the state college in Bozeman, nearly three hundred miles from the university in Missoula, distances that in those days of chugging Model Ts were far greater than they are today, and the young men and women of the Highline needed access to higher education that was closer to home. So a board was appointed, and a president hired, and classes were begun in church basements and whichever rooms the public schools could spare. The president offered a two-year curriculum in Latin and Greek, taught by himself. Then he hired a young man to teach chemistry, told him to build his own lab, and, by the way, to organize and coach a basketball team, which the young man did. The idea was that the graduates of the two-year curriculum would then transfer to the University of Minnesota, perhaps because of medical and other programs that wouldn't then have been available at the Montana universities. Everyone was so poor that some of the older professors remembered lending money to their students so they could stay in school.

Eventually, enrollment grew to a whopping five or six hundred students, and money was found to construct a couple of buildings from bricks salvaged from an abandoned military fort. After World War II, a new president arrived with his own ideas for Northern Montana College, which were to junk the Latin and Greek and add vocational programs in everything from automotive transmissions to flight instruction to cosmetology to teacher education. To accommodate teacher certification, the curriculum stretched to four years. By 1969, enrollment had grown to its all-time high of nearly fourteen hundred students. The vocational-minded president had departed, leaving behind his practical programs and part of an airplane, and a power struggle had replaced him in the president's office by an ex-professor of education. The idea now was to strengthen the four-year academic programs for accreditation, hence the need to hire assistant professors with PhDs.

Our young woman, mercifully unaware of all this history, walks up a sidewalk between stretches of lawn (the campus lawns are new, she'll learn; previously the grounds were grown over with shortgrass and sagebrush) and into Cowan Hall for the first time, where she hears her heels ring on the floors in the clean white light that floods through the tiers of single-pane windows. Most of the faculty and staff are gone for the summer, George Craig explains, as he introduces her to a small dark gnome of a woman who pokes her head from around her switchboard in a closet near the stairs. She turns out to be the possessor of the throaty voice. One of the English professors who is around is a Stephen Liu, who teaches Shakespeare and writes poetry (and will write more poetry, once he moves to the University of Nevada, Las Vegas, and isn't teaching quite so much freshman composition). There are five or six others in the English department, and they all teach freshman composition courses and the handful of literature courses leading to the BS degree in teacher education and to a tiny BA degree in English.

What can be accomplished in this place, wonders the young woman, whose idea of a college is the University of Missouri at Columbia. What can be imagined here, what will the future hold?

The future: she will often feel as though she has exchanged the myth of Ariadne and the labyrinth for the myth of Sisyphus. As teacher education programs shrink and vocational programs flourish and the job market continues to worsen, she and other liberal arts faculty will find themselves in a No Exit bastion of curriculum quarrels, campus politics, budget cuts, crises of all kinds. But no! They'll insist they're not rolling a rock uphill. They're fighting for their programs, for the liberal arts, in the face of ridicule from the other side of the campus: *What do some people think this college is all about! Where do they get the idea that college is about ideas, when everyone knows it's about job skills?*

One of her colleagues—the students call him Spiderman, for his strange lunging gait down the corridors of Cowan Hall—has a habit of beginning his sentences with, "At Yale, we used to . . ." to cries of derision. *This is not the Ivy League!*

While she herself—because the nearest university library is three hundred miles away, and it's the 1970s, with no Internet, only a clunky interlibrary loan system that may or may not produce xeroxed articles after a six-week wait—without quite knowing that she's doing it, she'll stop trying to keep current with her scholarship. Instead, she'll pick up the threads of fiction that she spun as an undergraduate. She'll write short stories about the isolated ranches and the silent people who live and struggle against weather and change and bankruptcy, she'll bare the bones of her people and the bones of the people they displaced. Oh, no, she won't let herself be buried alive. If her fiction seems light years distant in theme and tone from *Aspects of Juvenal in Ben Jonson's Comical Satires*, who better than the old satirist and the university-trained stepson of a London bricklayer to be looking over her shoulder?

But right now it's late July of 1969, and George Craig shows her around the campus and the town, takes her to dinner with his wife, then drops her off at the Havre Hotel where she can hear the coupling and uncoupling of boxcars while she thinks about the opportunity she's being offered and the risks that, as yet, are shadows on the margins of her thoughts. Although she knows that what can be seen in a single view is not all there is, she won't venture into those shadows, won't ask herself what will become of her marriage or whether she can survive the reassembling of the pieces of herself in the circle she seems to have traveled.

In the morning George Craig will drive her back to the airport in Great Falls and tell her that they can offer her $11,000 for ten months. He'll ask her what she thinks.

She says that she's got to talk it over with her husband.

Yes of course, he agrees, but his face falls, he thinks she's going to turn down the offer.

She already knows she will accept.

I

[I]t was the fear that in order to be what he might become he would have to cease to be what he had been, he would have to turn away from that place to which his flesh and his thoughts and his devotions belonged. —WENDELL BERRY, *The Memory of Old Jack*

IN THE SPRING OF 1944 my mother and father borrowed more money than they had ever seen and purchased the old home ranch on Spring Creek, in central Montana, that had been my great-grandfather's 1882 homestead. My father would be thirty-one in a few weeks, my mother had just turned thirty. I was four years old, my sister a toddler of eighteen months. We had been living on an alkali ranch in the sagebrush, down on the Judith River, and the move meant hay meadows and fresh water and good grazing for the cattle on the slopes of the mountains that overlooked the creek drainage, together with all the family associations with place, which even in 1944 were becoming emblematic. My great-grandfather had been one of the earliest homesteaders in central Montana, and it seemed that every shale hill and coulee, bend of the creek or grove of cottonwood trees, had its name and its position in the landscape of the family narrative.

Nearly seventy years later, I look back on that time and think how heartbreakingly young my mother and father were in 1944, with their two small daughters and their debt and their plans to deepen their roots on land where gnarled posts had been set and barbed wire strung on line fences by my great-grandfather and his sons, and where peonies and hollyhocks planted by my great-grandmother still bloomed every summer around the steps of the log ranch house where my father had been born. My parents dreamed of building up their herd of grade Hereford cows and calves, of constructing a two-bedroom house with modern improvements like electricity and telephone service, of repairing the corrals and barns and fences and clearing the underbrush that would, as my father said, make the ranch a *place* again.

The life my parents dreamed on the Spring Creek ranch was sheltered from the rest of the world by mountain ranges and distances and the slow pace of news, which came by radio, provided that somebody had bought batteries for the radio and the batteries hadn't run down. Or else the news came by a two- or three-day-old newspaper, delivered by the rural mail carrier, which had reported the Allied bombing of Europe and the liberation of France and the American bombing of Hiroshima and Nagasaki and the discovery of concentration camps, so far away that the ranch families of central Montana could keep their innocence.

Those ranch families had suffered, as did other Americans during World War II, from shortages and rationing. It was hard to get gasoline, hard to get tires, hard to find fresh meat and fresh eggs in the stores. But in 1944 most of those ranchers were putting up their hay with teams of horses and mowing machines and buck rakes and beaver slides, and they were planting gardens, as they always had done, and raising their own chickens and butchering their own meat. Most of them had never known the conveniences of electricity or refrigeration; they still pumped their water by hand and heated it on a wood stove. For bathing, a galvanized tub on the kitchen floor; for necessities, an outhouse. If they were lucky, they had a washing machine with a hand-turned agitator instead of a washboard and that same galvanized tub. Electricity? Not in the country, not until after the war. Telephones? My family hooked up to a party line in 1949. Television? Not until 1956.

Does it sound like a Wendell Berry dream? That self-contained little ranch, undefiled by technology, where everybody worked hard but everybody had enough to eat, where good grass grew in those hay meadows along the river, where cattle grazed all summer long on the slopes of the South Moccasin Mountains? Where entertainment, except for the huzzah and razzle-dazzle of county fair time, was conversation by lamplight around the supper table?

My father wanted no other life. Couldn't imagine anybody in his right mind wanting another life, couldn't understand why some of his uncles had followed the war work to California and settled there, slaving for wages and calling another man boss. At least when a man was his own boss, he could take off a day when he wanted to (not that my father ever did, not with hay to stack between rains and cows to milk and fences to be fixed, no rest all summer long, then no rest in the early Montana winters with teams to be harnessed to sleds and hay hauled to the cattle and horses, then in late winter and early spring the riding to look after the cattle calving on those same open slopes of the South Moccasin Mountains).

I have only the most fleeting memories of that first year on the Spring Creek ranch, but recently I discovered the diary that my mother's older sister, who had been teaching in southwest

Washington and come home for a visit, kept during the summer of 1944.

Doris & Jack [my parents] on a ranch deal, my aunt noted on May 13, 1944, and then, on July 10, after her school let out and she returned to Montana for her summer visit, *I rode herd on the kids. They were hoping I'd come. First time this summer I've been up river.*

It was the first time, in other words, that she had seen the Spring Creek ranch since my parents had purchased it. For my mother and father, that summer must have been frantically busy, between keeping up with the work on the alkali ranch and still getting the haying done on their new meadows. The rain my aunt reported in her diary had delayed the haying—they were still stacking the last of it in August—so she pitched in, helping wherever she could. From her diary entries, it is clear that she and my mother were working almost every day in the hayfields along with the usual cooking and cleaning and clothes washing and the care of two little girls. My mother must have been grateful for her sister's assistance. *How tired Doris looked tonight*, my aunt noted several times over the summer.

> *July 13: We put in half a day putting up hay.*
> *July 14: Jack went for a [hay] stacker. Took all day. Doris & I explored & picked berries & rhubarb.*
> *July 15: They worked all morning on the stacker. We got in a good whack at the hay in the afternoon.*
> *July 17: We finished stacking the field & moved the stacker after dinner. What a trip. Willow brush 10 feet high. Crossed Spring Creek & Little Judith River, [which flowed through the ranch and into the Big Judith River].*

The hay stacker was a teetering construction of poles and hand-sawed lumber, probably just taller than the willows, with a set of teeth that worked on a set of pulleys to carry a load of hay up the incline of the stacker and flip it on top of the growing haystack. Moving the stacker, all those ropes and poles and teeth and high creaking lumber behind a straining team of workhorses, across a creek knee-deep on the horses and across a deeper, swifter river, through willows and chokecherries that caught at the frame of the stacker and threatened to tip it over, was a tense operation of hours while the hay in the next meadow waited and ripened and overripened. Everyone's tempers would have been short. The horses probably got the worst of it.

July 22: Sat[urday]. The rope [on the hay stacker] snapped some tools into the air. Cut Jack's chin. Doris & I took him to the Dr. Had stitches.

I can just remember that day. One of those ranch thunderbolts with no warning. One minute all going well, the next minute the sudden snap of rope, the flash of metal, and my father's bleeding face. My mother and aunt probably packed the gash as best they could, loaded him into the old pickup, left the little girls with their grandmother, and headed for town as fast as they dared on wartime tires, with my father fuming because he wasn't driving, because he wasn't getting his haying done, probably swearing he was okay, no need for such a fuss, no need for stitches and a doctor's bill.

He had been lucky, of course. Lucky not to have been blinded. Or killed. And then what would have become of his wife and his mother and his little girls.

July 23: Sun[day]. Doris went for Jack. We [probably my aunt and my grandmother] hayed in the P.M. Got a nice stack started but cleared such a small patch of ground.
July 25: Doris hayed today. She wanted Jack to lay off & get Ma to come & care for the kids but Jack wouldn't lay off.

Of course not. He wouldn't lay off, he still had hay down, and already it was late July.

My aunt waits for nearly a week after the accident before she risks thinking about what might have been. Risks putting it in a few cautious words.

July 28: Jack's chin is healing fine. Tomorrow he hopes to get the bandage off. So glad it was no worse. It could have been really bad.
August 6: Sunday. Took another swing at the hay. Have about one day's work left I hope.
August 7: I'm taking care of the kids today while the rest go to town. Have only 3 weeks left [before her school starts again] & are they full. I don't feel like I've had any vacation.
August 12: We went to finish haying.

After the haying, my aunt went back to southwest Washington to teach school, but my mother continued her cycle of work, cooking three meals a day on a wood stove and washing every sheet and shirt and pair of blue jeans with water she had hand pumped and heated on that stove (washing them on a washboard until electricity came to the ranch after the war and she got a Maytag with an agitator and a wringer), and sprinkling and ironing all those clothes with irons heated on the wood stove, and feeding and watering her chickens and gathering and candling the eggs to be sold in town, and helping with the milking and separating the cream and making butter out of what wasn't sold in town, and weeding and watering her vegetable garden (more water to be hand pumped and carried), and all this in addition to working in the hayfields or the harvest fields. No wonder she was too tired to play with her little girls, or read to them, or do more than snap at them to behave themselves. My sister and I looked forward as much as she did to my aunt's summer visits.

My teacher grandmother, my mother's mother, had begun teaching me to read the summer I was three. From one of the rural schools she taught in, she brought home an outdated pre-primer about two spotted dogs named Nip and Tuck and showed me the letters and coached me in sounding out the words.

N-n-n-i-p-p-p!

Easy enough, even if the process seemed mechanical and boring.

Above a sentence or two of print on every page of the book about Nip and Tuck was an illustration of a world far beyond my sagebrush hills. What was I to think of neighborhoods where families lived in trim houses with spreading green lawns, and where spotted dogs danced in the spray of water from a hose as a father washed a car? A garden hose? Washing a car? What a concept!

I had never seen anyone wash a car, or do more than kick loose the gumbo mud that caked around the fenders of a pickup truck. Water, in my experience, spurted out of a pump with a handle. Or it ran in a muddy stream down an irrigation ditch that my dad would divert with a shovel to flow through rows of corn and peas and potatoes. Or it sparkled in the current of the river and dripped down the muzzles of the team of workhorses when they paused to drink. The odor of river water drew the cattle down from the hills and dyed their dark red darker where it eddied around their legs.

Water, precious and hard-come-by. And yet there were Nip and Tuck, cavorting down a paved sidewalk with the boy and girl who lived in the house with the picket fence in the shade of trees. What further surprises might the world hold?

Still, reading seemed pointless and lame, nothing like the luxurious out-of-body state of being read aloud to. But there I was, one afternoon, five or six years old and bored out of my mind, with nobody to play with but a toddler sister who needed a nap. I had a book and nobody had time to read it to me.

No, I can't read to you now. Maybe after milking. Maybe after supper. After the dishes are done. Not now. Go play.

The sun was shining. It was summertime, more work for everyone on a ranch. I wandered off across the yard with my book under my arm, barefoot, scabby kneed, and grumpy, the only person for miles with nothing to do. Around the house was trampled-down dry shortgrass, separated from the hay meadows by a dirt road and a grove of chokecherries. The book was a fourth-grade geography textbook, with a yellow cover, probably lifted from some school of my grandmother's. Its title was *Our Little Neighbors around the World at Work and Play*, which I'm certain of, because I still possess the book.

Well, what the. Give it a blankety-blank try.

What happened was a flash of unblinding.

In that new and unexpected light, I realized that I did not need to hear the sound of every separate letter, I did not need to mouth every word, in fact I did not need to pause on a word I did not understand. No, by golly, I could *flow*, absorbing whole lines, paragraphs, and pages as the lines and paragraphs and pages absorbed me. I think I realized something profound had happened, but I didn't stop to ponder, because I was *reading*.

On and on I read, about children in China and Mexico and the Philippines, while the hard Montana sunlight blazed down on the pages and made the letters dance. On and on and on. Glasses for my nearsightedness would be the next expense my parents somehow would have to scrape together the money to meet.

That evening, when my rancher grandmother said she had time now to read my book to me, I said, "Never mind, I already read it."

A silence of adults, eyes meeting over my head.

2

By the time my little sister and I enrolled in the Duck Creek School in 1949, a lot in ranch country had changed. For one thing, the terrible drought years of the 1920s and the depression of the 1930s had ended the hopes of thousands of young homesteaders, who lost their farms and ranches to debt and foreclosure. Montana lost a third of its population during those years, and over half of its rural schools. Then came World War II and another population shift, giving rural teachers like my favorite aunt the chance to move over to Washington State and earn twice the salary without having to shovel coal and carry water. Rural school boards searched high and low, but if they couldn't find a teacher, the school had to close.

Not that I understood anything about history or economics,

but I did overhear some of the anxious conversation—have you found a teacher yet? No, have you?

But the day came when my little sister and I, decked out in new dresses hand sewn by my mother and equipped with a new lunch box to share and new tablets and pencils and crayons, were driven up the precarious dirt road from the ranch and over several miles of graveled road to the Duck Creek School.

September in Montana can be dry and mild, and I remember our introduction to Duck Creek as very pleasant. The school was fresh from its fall cleaning, and the American flag floated from its pole, and the windows had been opened to the familiar odors of ripening wheat and creek water. So many novelties to experience: a hallway with hooks for our coats and a Redwing cooler that held drinking water, the long schoolroom with rows of desks in graduated sizes, the portraits of George Washington and Abraham Lincoln on the wall above the teacher's desk, and most enticing of all, a three-shelf bookcase that was the school's library.

Including my sister and me, nine pupils were enrolled in the Duck Creek School that fall: the three Anderson girls, who rode horseback down from their father's remote ranch in the foothills and stabled their horses in the ramshackle barn during the school day; Buzzie Huffine, a large and good-natured seventh-grader; Louise Snapp and her brother Billy, who were attending the Duck Creek School because their parents hadn't been able to find a teacher for their school; and Dixie Grover, who would be a first-grader with my sister. We all clattered around to decide which desks best accommodated our summer's growth of arms and legs, and I enjoyed stowing my new tablet and crayons in my desk and, at noon, sitting outside the school in one of the clanging swings to drink milk out of a thermos and trade sandwiches with Louise Snapp.

There were other pleasures. Games at recess that involved

kicking cans or choosing up sides and running back and forth with sticks from the woodpile. Taking turns carrying the water bucket across the gravel road in front of the school, over the stile, and down the trail to the spring in the cow pasture to fetch back water to pour into the Redwing cooler. I knew that my favorite aunt had taught at the Duck Creek School in the dim past—she'd actually taught the oldest Anderson girl as a first-grader—but I didn't know she had noted in her diary the day she had followed that same trail through the cow pasture to clean that same spring. I hadn't grasped the unspoken family assumption that I would follow in her and my mother's footsteps and teach in my own country school someday. But I was changing. The days when I thought of myself in third person were long past; wary of ridicule from listening adults, I no longer told myself out loud what I was thinking. I was on the cusp of a new awareness, seeing the world through my own eyes and no one else's, and my eyes were on that case of unread books. I wouldn't stop until I had finished every single book, and then I would start reading them over again.

Those days at Duck Creek sometimes seem as close and immediate and clear as the glass of those tall schoolhouse windows that looked across the trampled grass of the schoolyard to the graveled road angling north toward the Judith Mountains and eventually fading out of sight. The schoolroom itself was like a capsule in which routines were repeated day after day and nothing exciting happened, except the day the stubble field on the other side of the schoolyard caught fire and one of the Anderson girls jumped on her horse and tore off to get help from a neighbor while the teacher and Buzzie Huffine beat back the flames with shovels and sacks.

In the capsule of the schoolroom, with its pinewood floors and interlocking desks with lids that lifted over the clutter of our workbooks, as we scratched away with the steel pens that were passed out at penmanship time, and breathed the fumes of real ink, we lived in the present, with little suspicion of a future and no sense of the past as anything but remote. We didn't know that we were the last generation of children to dip our steel pens into our little bottles of reeking ink and practice slants and ovals on lined paper, according to the Palmer method, with admonitions from the teacher not to draw our ovals with our fingers (lest writers' cramp set in) but to keep our hands and wrists motionless and move our pens by rotating our forearms on our desks. As we obediently dipped our pens and rotated our forearms, we were anachronisms ranging in age from five to seventeen, but we didn't know it.

OUR TEACHER THAT FIRST year was a short-tempered redhead who drove out from Lewistown on Monday mornings, spent the week in the teacherage behind the schoolroom, and drove back to Lewistown on Friday afternoons to spend the weekend with her husband. Neighborhood gossip had it that she was teaching to keep ahead of his gambling debts. I can't remember any of the lessons she taught, although I do remember her scolding me for reading too fast, or not reading closely—"I was watching your eyes! They weren't moving back and forth across the lines! Read it again!"

She was right about the way my eyes moved on the page. I had taught myself to read in a kind of sweep, in the literary equivalent of bolting my food. I had been tested that summer by the county superintendent of schools so she could decide which grade I should be placed in, although discovering that I was reading at a twelfth-grade level and doing arithmetic at a third-grade level couldn't have been much help to her. It didn't matter to me when I was placed in fourth grade with two of the

Anderson girls and Billy Snapp. They couldn't keep up with me. I finished what I was assigned and then I reread one of the seventy or so books that made up the school library, or I sat and drew pictures, or I entertained myself with my elaborately imagined stories that spun through my head like an alternative life I was living. The redheaded teacher was the least of my worries.

I now suspect that I was the least of hers. If I wasn't going to pay attention to what she was trying to teach me, she may have decided I wasn't worth the bother. She hadn't wanted my little sister and me in her school in the first place. Like Louise and Billy Snapp, we belonged in another district, except that in our case our assigned school was situated on the other side of the Judith River, with no bridge for miles. But there we were in the Duck Creek School, and there was the redheaded teacher, and when my five-year-old sister threw up because the teacher yelled at her for forgetting the words on the page, she gave up on my sister, too. It wasn't until my sister started in a Lewistown school in the middle of fourth grade that anyone realized she had never learned to read at all.

Thanks to my valiant rancher grandmother, who drilled and drilled me, I learned the multiplication tables and I learned to spell. My rancher grandmother also cared deeply about the doings of people like Coronado and Cortez and de Soto and de Leon, and she tried to interest me in the string of firsts they seemed to have run up, like discovering the Mississippi River and the Fountain of Youth, but in that project she was never successful.

My sister and I attended the Duck Creek School for three and a half years. A well-meaning little woman with two sons of her own had followed the redheaded woman as our teacher, but it was during that final half year that we learned just how strange school could be.

It had looked as though we wouldn't find a teacher for that year at all. Then—hallelujah!—at the last possible minute, a neighboring ranch wife said she'd take the school. She'd been very ill—she wasn't sure she could do it—but yes, she thought she could. Everyone was very pleased; she was said to have been an excellent teacher before her illness.

Years later I wrote a short story about those few months with the teacher I called Mrs. Skaarda, and when the story was published in *The Georgia Review*, my sister and brother-in-law read it.

"She had to have made it up. These things couldn't have happened," said my brother-in-law.

"Oh yes they did," said my sister. "Oh yes they did."

Mrs. Skaarda, as I'll continue to call her, was a bird-boned little woman with an anxious face and eyes that searched our faces for reassurance as she told us how glad she was to be well again, and how much she looked forward to be spending the year with us. We were a depleted little group; the oldest Anderson girl had turned eighteen and given up on schooling, and Buzzie and his mother had moved to town after his father died, and the Snapps, miraculously, had found a teacher for their school, so Billy and Louise were gone. Besides my sister and me, that left only the other two Andersons and two new first-graders, a little girl I'll now call Jill, who seemed to have a bladder infection, and a little boy whom I called Forby in my short story.

All of us except Jill and Forby were surprised when Mrs. Skaarda didn't assign us schoolwork, but instead began a rambling monologue from which, she said, she hoped we learned more than we would from lessons. What she wanted us to know was that she had enemies. There had been professors when she was in college, the director of a theater group she had belonged to, a man who had taught her niece so badly in a city school, her sister-in-law—

It turned out that her father-in-law had been dying of cancer. Mrs. Skaarda's voice shook as she told us how cancer had its own terrible smell, so putrid and horrible that only she, of the whole family, could bear to sit in the same room with him. Others in the family, she said, didn't really *care* that he was dying.

At this point Jill flung herself out of her seat and tore through the schoolroom, banging doors behind her, on her way to the outhouse.

Mrs. Skaarda went on talking about her father-in-law. Her voice trembled. "I sat up with him all night. I held his hand. No one else would stay with him. He died about three o'clock in the morning. Did you know that dead bodies fart?"

We sat in rapt silence, all but Forby, who was coloring with his black crayon.

As the fall grew chillier and the oil stove had to be lit, Mrs. Skaarda grew fearful. After a few days of ordinary lessons, her eyes searched the classroom and came to rest on the stove.

"If it exploded, it would kill us all," her voice broke the silence, and we all looked up, blinking in the sunlight that strained through the frosted windows. All but Forby, that is, who kept coloring with his black crayon. "My desk is on the far side of the room, and they might be able to identify my body. But most of you would be mutilated beyond recognition."

"If it exploded, I'd jump up and run," said one of the Anderson girls.

"You wouldn't have time to run," said Mrs. Skaarda.

For the rest of the week we watched the oil heater and breathed as tentatively as we could. Mrs. Skaarda, however, had begun to worry about Jill, who continued to punctuate her runs to the outhouse with slammed doors.

"She's been wetting her panties," said Mrs. Skaarda. "I can smell her."

Slam! went another door behind one of Jill's desperate dashes.

"Bang! Bang!" Mrs. Skaarda shouted at the slammed door. "There go the British!"

We never knew what became of Jill. She simply stopped attending school. It is possible that Mrs. Skaarda complained to her parents, or more likely to the neighbors who had hired her parents for fall work. Or maybe Jill told her parents what was happening. Or maybe not, maybe her family just moved away. When I look back over those years, I'm struck by how little any of us told our parents about what was happening at school. We chattered at home about who said what smart thing on the playground and what smart thing got said back, but we didn't tell that my sister threw up when the redheaded teacher yelled at her, or that the redheaded teacher once sneaked up behind me and pummeled me with her fists for no reason I ever knew, and we didn't tell about Mrs. Skaarda until long after the fact.

Did our complicit silence grow out of our sense of the school-room as a capsule in which we were suspended from the day-to-day of the rest of the world? As I reread my short story, I am struck by what I kept of the facts and what I changed: my own role in the Forby episode, for example.

Because, after Jill vanished, Mrs. Skaarda turned her attention on Forby. "There's something the matter with him," she whispered to the rest of us. "Why does he always color with his black crayon?"

Forby kept coloring, and Mrs. Skaarda's worries grew. "If he were ever to lose control, it would take more than any one of us to subdue him," she confided in her troubled whisper. "The insane have strength beyond all normal measures. That's what I'm afraid of. That he'll snap and overpower us all."

By this time every pair of eyes in school was glued on Forby. Could we possibly have believed the child was insane? I only know that Forby gradually looked up from his crayons to find a wall of suspicion around him. At recess he was no longer chosen on anyone's side in games. He took to hovering at a distance of a few yards, pawing with his overshoes at the sod.

"Get away!" somebody might bellow across a few yards of prairie grass at uncomprehending Forby in his thick coat and cap. "Keep away from us!"

"Go away!"

From the first, Forby made no defense, withdrawing more deeply into himself when we darted at him, threatening. How long did our bullying go on? Could it have been for days? And what part did I play, what am I masking from myself by my use of the collective "we," my sheltering in our tiny group? I do remember that the day Forby finally broke and ran, I ran after him with everybody else, and just as we saw we were going to corner him by the barbed wire fence that separated the school-yard from the neighboring grain field, Forby flung himself on that fence and set the wires vibrating for yards.

At that precise moment, Forby's mother showed up. She broke into a run with her coat flapping about her legs, plucked Forby off the barbed wire, and carried him back toward the school.

Here my memory darkens. I cannot see Forby lolling on her shoulder as she opens the door of the school, I cannot see her carrying him to her car. Her arrival seemed to me at the time as just one more unlikely event. Was it in fact a complete non sequitur, or had she gotten wind of the bullying and come to look into it? I do know that I was eleven and the Anderson girls probably twelve and fourteen, old enough to know we shouldn't have been picking on a six-year-old.

In my short story, my point-of-view character is a revision of myself as Forby's prime persecutor, whose motive is to win Mrs. Skaarda's approval. I can gloss my revision as a way of telling the story of a scapegoat, or I can ponder the story I was avoiding, because at the time, the last thing on my mind was Mrs. Skaarda's approval. In retrospect, I realize that growing between us was the perverse flower of antagonism that I would feel toward various teachers and professors even through graduate school. Mrs. Skaarda and I argued about the interpretations of stories in school readers. We argued about the correct position of one's fingers on piano keys (I was taking piano lessons from the redoubtable Miss Pennock in Lewistown, who insisted on a certain finger curvature and wrist position that Mrs. Skaarda considered unnecessary and ungraceful). We argued about the significance of ancient Mayan human sacrifice (a detail I retained in my short story was that she lent me a book on the topic that gave me nightmares). Mouthy and obnoxious, that was me—or, at least, how Mrs. Skaarda probably saw me.

Our days at Duck Creek were coming to an end. The first winter blizzard hit just as my parents began the move from the ranch on the river to the ranch they had bought in the foothills of the Snowy Mountains, close enough to Lewistown that my sister and I, and the new little sister, ten years younger than I, could attend town schools and eventually go to high school without having to board away from home. What with the perils of bad roads and blowing snow and the uncertainties of starting over, my father and mother would have had more on their minds than Mrs. Skaarda and the shadows only she perceived.

But I missed a day or two of school, toward the end of that last term, and my little sister uncharacteristically came home with a story about Mrs. Skaarda, who had gathered her dwindling little flock about her and told them that Mary hated her.

"But you," she smiled through her tears, hugging my sister. "You're so sweet. You'd do anything for me."

THE DUCK CREEK SCHOOL couldn't have stayed open for more than another year or two, if that. For a long time it sat empty by the side of the road, its long row of windows filmed with dust, until somebody hauled it off to use as a granary. Mrs. Skaarda got a job teaching in an elementary school in a small town and won a Teacher of the Year award. The youngest Anderson girl gave high school a try and dropped out after a few months. Forby grew up to farm his father's land. Jill might as well have dropped off the face of the earth, as far as any of us ever knew.

A fourth-grade teacher in Lewistown spotted my sister's illiteracy and taught her to read. I started high school with a curious assortment of knowledge and skills—the multiplication tables, an unwilling suspicion that de Soto, de Leon, Cortez, and Coronado really mattered, and the ability to read faster than anyone my teachers had ever encountered—and found in those teachers a whole new set of assumptions about what a girl ought to learn, and how she ought to learn it.

SEVERAL YEARS AGO MY sister and I detoured off the highway, now a paved road, and visited the granary that once had been the Duck Creek School. It tilted off its foundation with its desks still bolted to its hardwood floor and a clutter of forgotten primers and workbooks discarded in the chaff. My sister picked up one of the readers as a keepsake, then changed her mind, laid it back down on the floor, and took a few pictures instead. It seemed the right thing to do. Those pictures show us in our bright summer clothing, a couple of aliens in a dusty time capsule. And yet that time capsule, lopsided and askew, once had been solid and real and eternal. Mrs. Skaarda was right: we had learned a great deal at Duck Creek that had nothing to do with lessons.

3

DECEMBER 1958. I lie on my back on an examination table in a Missoula clinic while the middle-aged doctor whose name I found in the Yellow Pages inserts his speculum and takes a look. He turns to the sink and washes his hands.

"Yes, you're pregnant," he says. "Congratulations, Mommy."

His confirmation settles over me like a fog that won't lift. Myself I can manage for, but for myself and *it*?

After I get dressed, he says, "I'll want to see you again in a month, Mommy."

If he calls me Mommy again, I will break his glasses and grind them in his face, grind them until he has no face. I will kick him right in his obscene fat paunch. I will bury my foot in his disgusting flesh.

I walk through the glass doors and between the shoveled banks of snow to the parking lot where my young husband waits in the car.

"You're not, are you?" he says.

"Yes."

"Yes, you're not?"

"Yes, I am! Jeez!"

His feelings are hurt. But he persists: "I just don't think you are. I just don't see how you could be."

He has a theory on the correct use of condoms, a theory considerably more flexible than the one outlined by the doctor I visited just before our marriage three months ago, and which he has been arguing with increasing anxiety ever since I missed my second period. I stare out the car window at the back of the clinic while he expounds on his theory for the zillionth time. What difference does it make now? Why can't he shut up? If I have to listen to him much longer, I will kill him, too.

At last, even his arguments wear thin against the irrefutable fact. As he turns the key in the ignition his eyes are deep with fear.

"But I'll stand by you," he promises.

WHY GET MARRIED at eighteen?

When you get married, you can move into married student housing. It's a shambles, it's a complex of converted World War II barracks known as the Strips, it's so sorry the wind blows through the cracks around the windows and it lacks hot-water heaters and electric stoves, but at least it's not the dormitory, which is otherwise the required residence of all women at the University of Montana. Although no such regulations apply to male students, single women must be signed in and ready for bed check by ten o'clock on weeknights and one on weekends. No alcohol, no phones in rooms. Women must not be reported on campus in slacks or shorts (unless they can prove they are on their way to a physical education class), and on Sundays they may not appear except in heels, hose, and hat. A curious side effect of marriage, however, is that the responsibility for one's virtue is automatically transferred from the dean of women to one's husband. Miss Maurine Clow never does bed checks or beer checks in the Strips.

When you get married, you can quit making out in the back seat of a parked car and go to bed in a bed. All young women in 1958 like sex. Maybe their mothers had headaches and hang-ups, but *they* are normal, healthy women with normal, healthy desires, and they know the joy they will find in their husbands' arms will—well, be better than making out, which, though none of us will admit it, is getting to be boring. We spend hours shivering with our clothes off in cars parked in Pattee Canyon in subzero weather, groping and being groped and feeling embarrassed when other cars crunch by in the snow, full of onlookers with craning necks, and worrying about the classes we're not attending because making out takes so much time. We are normal, healthy women with normal healthy desires if we have to die to prove it. Nobody has ever said out loud that she would like to go to bed and *get it over with* and get on with something else.

There's another reason for getting married at eighteen, but it's more complicated.

$\sim$

By getting married I have eluded Dean Maurine Clow only to fall into the hands of in-laws.

"We have to tell the folks," my husband insists. "They'll want to know."

His letter elicits the predictable long-distance phone call from his folks. I make him answer it. While he talks to them I rattle dishes in the kitchen, knowing exactly how they look, his momma and his daddy in their suffocating Helena living room hung with mounted elk antlers and religious calendars, their heads together over the phone, their faces wreathed in big grins at his news.

"They want to talk to you," he says finally. Then, "Come on!"

I take the phone with fear and hatred. "Hello?"

"Well!!!" My mother-in-law's voice carols over the miles. "I guess this is finally the end of college for you!"

A WEEK AFTER CHRISTMAS I lean against the sink in my mother's kitchen at the ranch and watch her wash clothes.

She uses a Maytag washing machine with a wringer and a monotonous, daylong chugging motor, which, she often points out, is a damn sight better than a washboard. She starts by filling the tub with boiling water and soap flakes. Then she agitates her whites for twenty minutes, fishes them out with her big fork, and feeds them sheet by sheet into the wringer. After she rinses them by hand, she reverses the wringer and feeds them back through, creased and steaming hot, and carries them out to the clothesline to freeze dry. By this time the water in the tub has cooled off enough for the colors. She'll keep running through her loads until she's down to the blue jeans and the water is thick and greasy. My mother has spent twenty-five years of Mondays on the washing.

I know I have to tell her I'm pregnant.

She's talking about college, she's quoting my grandmother, who believes that every woman should be self-sufficient. Even though I'm married now, even though I had finished only one year at the University of Montana before I got married, my grandmother has agreed to lend me what I need for tuition and books. Unlike my in-laws, who have not hesitated to tell me I should go to work as a typist or a waitress to support my husband through college (after all, he will be supporting me for the rest of my life), my grandmother believes I should get my own credentials.

My mother and grandmother talk about a teaching certificate as if it were a gold ring that, if I could just grab it, would entitle the two of them to draw a long breath of relief. Normally I hate to listen to their talk. They don't even know you can't get a two-year teaching certificate now, you have to go the full four years.

But beyond the certificate question, college has become something that I never expected and cannot explain: not something to grab and have done with but a door opening, a glimpse of an endless passage and professors who occasionally beckon from far ahead—like lovely, elderly Marguerite Ephron, who lately has been leading four or five of us through the *Aeneid*. Latin class has been my sanctuary for the past few months; Latin has been my solace from conflict that otherwise has left me as steamed and agitated as my mother's whites, now churning away in the Maytag: Latin in part because it is taught by Mrs. Ephron, always serene, endlessly patient, mercilessly thorough, who teaches at the university while Mr. Ephron works at home, in a basement full of typewriters with special keyboards, on the translations of obscure clay tablets.

So I've been accepting my grandmother's money under false pretenses. I'm not going to spend my life teaching around Fergus County in the rural schools the way she did, the way my mother would have if she hadn't married my father. I've married my husband under false pretenses, too; he's a good fly-fishing Helena boy who has no idea in the world of becoming a Mr. Ephron. But, subversive as a foundling in a fairy tale, I have tried to explain none of my new aspirations to my mother or grandmother or, least of all, to my husband and his parents, who are mightily distressed as it is by my borrowing money for my own education.

"—and it's all got to be paid back, you'll be starting your lives in *debt!*"

"—the important thing is to get him through, *he's* the one who's got to go out and face the world!"

"—what on earth do you think you'll do with your education?"

And now all the argument is pointless, the question of teaching certificate over quest for identity, the importance of my husband's future over mine, the relentless struggle with the in-laws over what is most mine, my self. I'm done for, knocked out of the running by the application of a faulty condom theory.

"Mom," I blurt, "I'm pregnant."

She gasps. And before she can let out that breath, a frame of memory freezes of her poised over her rinse tub, looking at me through the rising steam and the grinding wringer. Right now I'm much too miserable to wonder what she sees when she looks at me: her oldest daughter, her bookish child, the daydreamer, the one she usually can't stand, the one who takes everything too seriously, who will never learn to take no for an answer. Thin and strong and blue-jeaned, bespectacled and crop haired, this girl could pass for fifteen right now and won't be able to buy beer in grocery stores for years without showing her driver's license. This girl who is too miserable to look her mother in the face, who otherwise might see in her mother's eyes the years of blight and disappointment. She does hear what her mother says:

"Oh, Mary, no!"

My mother was an unwanted child. The fourth daughter of a homesteading family racked by drought and debt, she was only a year old when the sister nearest her in age died of a cancerous tumor. She was only two years old when the fifth and last child, the cherished boy, was born. She was never studious like her older sisters nor, of course, was she a boy, and she was never able to find her own ground to stand on until she married.

Growing up, I heard her version often, for my mother was given to a kind of continuous oral interpretation of herself and her situation. Standing over the sink or stove, hoeing the garden, running her sewing machine with the permanent angry line deepening between her eyes, she talked. Unlike the stories our grandmothers told, which, like fairy tales, narrated the events of the past but avoided psychological speculation ("Great-great-aunt Somebody-or-other was home alone making soap when the Indians came, so she waited until they got close enough, and then she threw a ladle of lye on them . . ."), my mother's dwelt on the motives behind the darkest family impulses.

"Ma never should have had me. It was her own fault. She never should have had me if she didn't want me."

"But then you wouldn't have been born!" I interrupted, horrified at the thought of not being.

"Wouldn't have mattered to me," she said. "I'd never have known the difference."

What I cannot remember today is whom my mother was telling her story to. Our grandmothers told their stories to my little sisters and me, to entertain us, but my mother's bitter words flowed past us like a river current past small, ignored onlookers who eavesdropped from its shores. I remember her words, compulsive, repetitive, spilling out over her work—for she was always working—and I was awed by her courage. What could be less comprehensible than not wanting to be? More fearsome than annihilation?

Nor can I remember enough about the circumstances of my mother's life during the late 1940s and the early 1950s to know why she was so angry, why she was so compelled to deconstruct her childhood. Her lot was not easy. She had married into a close-knit family that kept to itself. She had her husband's mother on her hands all her life, and on top of the normal isolation and hard work of a ranch wife of those years, she had to provide home schooling for her children.

And my father's health was precarious, and the ranch was failing. The reality of that closed life along the river bottom became more and more attenuated by the outward reality of banks and interest rates and the shifting course of agribusiness. She was touchy with money worries. She saw the circumstances of her sisters' lives grow easier as her own grew harder. Perhaps these were reasons enough for rage.

I recall my mother in her middle thirties through the telescoped eye of the child that distorts the intentions of parents and enlarges them to giants. Of course she was larger than life. Unlike my father, with his spectrum of ailments, she was never sick. She was never hospitalized in her life for any reason but childbirth, never came down with anything worse than a cold. She lugged the armloads of wood and buckets of water and slops and ashes that came with cooking and washing and ironing in a kitchen with a wood range and no plumbing; she provided the endless starchy meals of roast meat and potatoes and gravy; she kept salads on her table and fresh or home-canned vegetables at a time when iceberg lettuce was a town affectation.

She was clear skinned, with large gray eyes that often seemed fixed on some point far beyond our familiar slopes and cutbanks. And even allowing for the child's telescoped eye, she was a tall woman who thought of herself as oversized. She was the tallest of her sisters. "*As big as Doris* is what they used to say about me!"

Bigness to her was a curse. "You big ox!" she would fling at me over some altercation with my little sister. True to the imperative that is handed down through the generations, I in turn bought my clothes two sizes too large for years.

All adult ranch women were fat. I remember hardly a woman out of her teens in those years who was not fat. The few exceptions were the women who had, virtually, become a third sex by taking on men's work in the fields and corrals; they might stay as skinny and tough in their Levi's as hired hands.

But women who remained women baked cakes and cream pies and breads and sweet rolls with the eggs from their own chickens and the milk and butter and cream from the cows they milked, and they ate heavily from appetite and from fatigue and from the monotony of their isolation. They wore starched cotton print dresses and starched aprons and walked ponderously beside their whiplash husbands. My mother, unless she was going to be riding or helping in the hayfields, always wore those shapeless, starched dresses she sewed herself, always cut from the same pattern, always layered over with an apron.

What was she so angry about? Why was her forehead kneaded permanently into a frown? It was a revelation for me one afternoon when she answered a knock at the screen door, and she smiled, and her voice lifted to greet an old friend of hers and my father's from their single days. Color rose in her face, and she looked pretty as she told him where he could find my father. Was that how outsiders always saw her?

Other ranch women seemed cheerful enough on the rare occasions when they came in out of the gumbo. Spying on them as they sat on benches in the shade outside the horticulture house at the county fair or visited in the cabs of trucks at rodeos, I wondered if these women, too, were angry when they were alone with only their children to observe them. What secrets lay behind those vast placid, smiling faces, and what stories could their children tell?

My mother believed that her mother had loved her brother best and her older sisters next best. "He was always The Boy and they were The Girls, and Ma was proud of how well they did in school," she explained again and again to the walls, the stove, the floor she was mopping, "and I was just Doris. I was average."

Knowing how my grandmother had misjudged my mother, I felt guilty about how much I longed for her visits. I loved my grandmother and her fresh supply of stories about the children who went to the schools she taught, the games they played, and the books they read. But my mother's resentment whitened in intensity during the weeks before a visit from my grandmother, smoldered during the visit itself, and flared up again as soon as my grandmother was safely down the road to her next school. "I wonder if she ever realizes she wouldn't even have any grand-children if I hadn't got married and had some kids! *The Girls* never had any kids! Some people should never have kids! Some people should never get married!"

With a child's logic, I thought she was talking about me. I thought I was responsible for her anger. I was preoccupied for a long time with a story I had read about a fisherman who was granted three wishes; he had used his wishes badly, but I was sure I could do better, given the chance. I thought a lot about how I would use three wishes, how I would use their potential for lifting me out of the present.

"What would you wish for, if you had three wishes?" I prod-ded my mother.

She turned her faraway gray eyes on me, as though she had not been ranting about The Girls the moment before. "I'd wish you'd be good," she said.

That was what she always said, no matter how often I asked her. With everything under the sun to wish for, that unfailing answer was a perplexity and a worry.

I was my grandmother's namesake, and I was a bookworm

like my mother's older sisters. Nobody could pry my nose out of a book to do my chores, even though I was marked to be the outdoor-working child, even though I was supposed to be my father's boy.

Other signs that I was not a boy arose to trouble us both and account, I thought, for my mother's one wish.

"Mary's getting a butt on her just like a girl," she remarked one night as I climbed out of the tub. Alarmed, I craned my neck to see what had changed about my eight-year-old buttocks.

"Next thing, you'll be mooning in the mirror and wanting to pluck your eyebrows like the rest of 'em," she said.

"I will not," I said doubtfully.

I could find no way through the contradiction. On the one hand, I was a boy (except that I also was a bookworm), and my chores were always in the barns and corrals, never the kitchen. *You don't know how to cook on a wood stove?* my mother-in-law was to cry in disbelief. *And you grew up on a ranch?*

To act like a boy was approved; to cry or show fear was to invite ridicule. *Sissy! Big bellercalf!* On the other hand, I was scolded for hanging around the men, the way ranch boys did. I was not a boy (my buttocks, my vanity). What was I?

"Your dad's boy," my mother answered comfortingly when I asked her. She named a woman I knew. "Just like Hazel. Her dad can't get along without her."

Hazel was a tough, shy woman who rode fences and pulled calves and took no interest in the country dances or the "running around" her sisters did on weekends. Hazel never used lipstick or permed her hair; she wore it cut almost like a man's. Seen at the occasional rodeo or bull sale in her decently pressed pearl-button shirt and new Levi's, she stuck close to her dad. Like me, Hazel apparently was not permitted to hang around the men.

What Hazel did not seem interested in was any kind of fun,

and a great resolve arose in me that, whatever I was, I was going to have . . . whatever it was. I would get married, even if I wasn't supposed to.

~

But my mother had another, darker reason to be angry with me, and I knew it. The reason had broken over me suddenly the summer I was seven and had been playing, on warm afternoons, in a rain barrel full of water. Splashing around, elbows and knees knocking against the side of the barrel, I enjoyed the rare sensation of being wet all over. My little sister, four, came and stood on tiptoe to watch. It occurred to me to boost her into the barrel with me.

My mother burst out of the kitchen door and snatched her back.

"What are you trying to do, kill her?" she shouted.

I stared back at her, wet, dumbfounded.

Her eyes blazed over me, her brows knotted at their worst. "And after you'd drowned her, I suppose you'd have slunk off to hide somewhere until it was all over!"

It had never crossed my mind to kill my sister, or that my mother might think I wanted to. (Although I had, once, drowned a setting of baby chicks in a rain barrel.) But that afternoon, dripping in my underpants, goose bumped and ashamed, I watched her carry my sister into the house, and then I did go off to hide until it was, somehow, all over, for she never mentioned it at dinner.

The chicks had been balls of yellow fuzz, and I had been three. I wanted them to swim. I can just remember catching a chick and holding it in the water until it stopped squirming and then laying it down to catch a fresh one. I didn't stop until I had drowned the whole dozen and laid them out in a sodden yellow row.

What the mind refuses to allow to surface is characterized by a suspicious absence. Of detail, of associations. Memories skirt the edge of nothing. There is for me about this incident that suspicious absence. What is being withheld?

Had I, for instance, given my mother cause to believe I might harm my sister? Children have done such harm, and worse. What can be submerged deeper, denied more vehemently, than the murderous impulse? At four, my sister was a tender, trusting little girl with my mother's wide gray eyes and brows. A younger sister of an older sister. A good girl. Mommy's girl.

What do I really know about my mother's feelings toward her own dead sister? Kathryn's dolls had been put away; my mother was never allowed to touch them.

"I'll never, never love one of my kids more than another!" she screamed at my father in one of her afternoons of white rage. The context is missing.

DURING THE GOOD YEARS, when cattle prices were high enough to pay the year's bills and a little extra, my mother bought wallpaper out of a catalog and stuck it to her lumpy walls. She enameled her kitchen white, and she sewed narrow strips of cloth she called "drapes" to hang at the sides of her windows. She bought a stiff tight cylinder of linoleum at Sears, Roebuck in town and hauled it home in the back of the pickup and unrolled it in a shiny flowered oblong in the middle of her splintery front room floor.

Occasionally I would find her sitting in her front room on her "davenport," which she had saved for and bought used, her lap full of sewing and her forehead relaxed out of its knot. For a moment there was her room around her as she wanted it to look: the clutter subdued, the new linoleum mopped and quivering under the chair legs that held down its corners, the tension of the opposing floral patterns of wallpaper, drapes, and slipcovers held in brief, illusory harmony by the force of her vision.

How hard she tried for her daughters! Over the slow thirty miles of gumbo and gravel we drove to town every summer for dentist appointments at a time when pulling teeth was still a more common remedy than filling them, when our own father and his mother wore false teeth before they were thirty.

During the good years, we drove the thirty miles for piano lessons. An upright Kimball was purchased and hauled home in the back of the pickup. Its carved oak leaves and ivories dominated the front room, where my mother found time to "sit with us" every day as we practiced. With a pencil she pointed out the notes she had learned to read during her five scant quarters in normal school, and made us read them aloud. "F sharp!" she would scream over the throb of the Maytag in the kitchen as one of us pounded away.

She carped about bookworms, but she located the dim old Carnegie library in town and got library cards for us even though, as country kids, we weren't strictly entitled to them. After that, trips home from town with sacks of groceries included armloads of library books. Against certain strictures she could be counted on. When, in my teens, I came home with my account of the new book the librarian kept in her desk drawer and refused to check out to me, my mother straightened her back as I knew she would. "She thinks she can tell one of my kids what she can read and what she can't read?"

On our next visit to the library, she marched up the stone steps and into the mote-filled sanctum with me.

The white-haired librarian glanced up inquiringly.

"You got *From Here to Eternity*?"

The librarian looked at me, then at my mother. Without a word she reached into her drawer and took out a heavy volume. She stamped it and handed it to my mother, who handed it to me.

How did she determine that books and dentistry and piano

lessons were necessities for her daughters, and what battles did she fight for them as slipping cattle prices put even a gallon of white enamel paint or a sheet of new linoleum beyond her reach?

Disaster followed disaster on the ranch. An entire season's hay crop lost to a combination of ancient machinery that would not hold together and heavy rains that would not let up. A whole year's calf crop lost because the cows had been pastured in timber that had been logged, and when they ate the pine needles from the downed tops, they spontaneously aborted. As my father grew less and less able to face the reality of the downward spiral, what could she hope to hold together with her pathetic floral drapes and floral slipcovers?

BUNDLED IN COATS and overshoes in the premature February dark, our white breaths as one, my mother and I huddle in the shadow of the chicken house. By moonlight we watch the white-tail deer that have slipped down out of the timber to feed from the haystack a scant fifty yards away. Cautiously I raise my father's rifle to my shoulder. I'm not all that good a marksman, I hate the inevitable explosive crack, but I brace myself on the corner of the chicken house and sight carefully and remember to squeeze. Ka-crack!

Eight taupe shapes shoot up their heads and spring for cover. A single mound remains in the snow near the haystack. By the time my mother and I have climbed through the fence and trudged up to the haystack, all movement from the doe is reflexive. "Nice and fat," says my mother.

Working together with our butcher knives, we lop off her scent glands and slit her and gut her and save the heart and liver in a bucket for breakfast. Then, each taking a leg, we drag her down the field, under the fence, around the chicken house, and into the kitchen, where we will skin her out and butcher her.

We are two mid-twentieth-century women putting meat on the table for the next few weeks. Neither of us has ever had a hunting license, and if we did, hunting season is closed, but we're serene about what we're doing. "Eating our hay, aren't they?" says my mother. "We're entitled to a little venison. The main thing is not to tell anybody what we're doing."

AND THE PREGNANT eighteen-year-old? What about her?

In June of 1959 she sits up in the hospital bed, holding in her arms a small warm scrap whose temples are deeply dented from the forceps. She cannot remember birthing him, only the long hours alone before the anesthetic took over. She feels little this morning, only a dull worry about the money, money, money for college in the fall.

The in-laws are a steady, insistent, increasingly frantic chorus of disapproval over her plans. *But, Mary! Tiny babies have to be kept warm!* her mother-in-law keeps repeating, pathetically, ever since she was told about Mary's plans for fall quarter.

But, Mary! How can you expect to go to college and take good care of a husband and a baby?

Finally, *We're going to put our foot down!*

She knows that somehow she has got to extricate herself from these sappy folks. About the baby, she feels only a mild curiosity. Life where there was none before. The rise and fall of his tiny chest. She has him on her hands now. She must take care of him.

Why not an abortion?

Because the thought never crossed her mind. Another suspicious absence, another voice for memory to skirt. What she knew about abortion was passed around the midnight parties in the girls' dormitory: *You drink one part turpentine to two parts sugar.* Or was it the other way around. *Two parts turpentine to one part sugar. You drink gin in a hot bath . . .*

She has always hated the smell of gin. It reminds her of the pine needles her father's cattle ate, and how their calves were born shallow-breathed and shriveled, and how they died. She knows a young married woman who begged her husband to hit her in the stomach and abort their fourth child.

Once, in her eighth month, the doctor had shot her a look across his table. "If you don't want this baby," he said, "I know plenty of people who do."

"I want it," she lied.

No, but really. What is to become of this eighteen-year-old and her baby?

Well, she's read all the sentimental literature they shove on the high school girls. She knows how the plot is supposed to turn out.

Basically, she has two choices.

One, she can invest all her hopes for her own future in this sleeping scrap. Son, it was always my dream to climb to the stars. Now the tears of joy spring at the sight of you with your college diploma . . .

Even at eighteen, she can't stand such lilylicking.

Or two, she can abandon the baby and the husband and become really successful and really evil. This is the more attractive version of the plot, but she doesn't really believe in it. Nobody she knows has tried it. It seems as out of reach from ordinary daylight Montana as Joan Crawford or the Duchess of Windsor or the moon. As she lies propped in bed with the sleeping scrap in her arms, looking out over the dusty downtown rooftops settling into noon in the waning Eisenhower years, she knows very well that Joan Crawford will never play the story of her life.

What then? What choice is left to her?

What outcome could possibly be worth all this uproar? Her husband is on the verge of tears these days; he's only twenty himself, and he had no idea what trouble he was marrying into, his parents pleading and arguing and threatening, even his brothers and their wives chiming in with their opinions, even the minister getting into it, even the neighbors, and meanwhile his wife's grandmother firing off red-hot letters from her side, meanwhile his wife's mother refusing to budge an inch—united, those two women are as formidable as a pair of rhinoceroses, though of course he has no idea in the world what it took to unite them.

All this widening emotional vortex over whether or not one Montana girl will finish college. What kind of genius would she have to be to justify it all? Will it be enough that, thirty years later, she will raise her head from a desk in an office in a small state college and realize that she has read approximately 16,250 freshman English essays out of an estimated lifetime total of 32,000?

Will it be enough over the years, that she remembers the frozen frame of her mother's face over the rinse tub that day after Christmas in 1958 and wonders whether she can do as much for her son as was done for her? Or that she wonders whether she really lied when she said, *I want it*?

Will it be enough? What else is there?

4

THAT SON HAS NOT spoken to me in over twenty-five years.

I reread the sentence I have just written and try and fail to connect the separate words with what they mean. Too many meanings, too many years. I believe there is pain in this world that is never healed, no matter how many years pass, but not this pain, not for me. What I feel, behind the bare words, is really more of an apprehension. What loose ends, what dirty secrets? What gargoyle struggles to open her eroded eyes and flap into the light? If I write another sentence, will I begin to grieve? What if I don't?

IT WAS THE FALL of 1974, and the Bertolucci film *Last Tango in Paris* finally had come to a movie theater in Havre, Montana.

My son, Jack, was beside himself to see it. Alas, *Last Tango* was X-rated, and Jack was only fourteen.

Jack and his best friend, Sean Prentiss, were big movie buffs, and they had worked out a system to get themselves into R-rated movies, which required parental permission. At first Mrs. Prentiss and I, worn down by pleas and promises from our sons, would phone the manager of the movie theater and give our permission for the boys to see whatever film they had set their hearts on. After a few months, however, there was a change of policy at the theater. How was the manager supposed to know who was making those phone calls? He wanted to see a handwritten note. So for a while we wrote notes. But then another change in policy, or perhaps a stiffening of the manager's resolve. He required our *personal* permission; and so, grumbling, Mrs. Prentiss and I would take turns driving down to the movie theater and glaring at the cashier while our sons' tickets were purchased. Anything for a few hours' peace and quiet.

X-rated, however, meant there was no question of parental permission. If you weren't eighteen, you didn't get in to see *Last Tango in Paris*.

Although every high school kid in town had tried and failed to sneak in (the problem was, the assistant principal at the local high school was moonlighting as a ticket-taker at the theater, and of course he recognized them all), Jack just couldn't believe his tried-and-true tactics of carping and whining and otherwise driving me crazy wouldn't somehow get him in to see the film. He hung around my desk while I was trying to grade papers, arguing with me about censorship and patriarchy and oppression, until I flung down my pen and threw up my hands.

"It doesn't matter whether I agree with you or not! The damned film is X-rated, and I can't do a thing to get you in to see it, short of dressing you in my clothes and my wig and giving you my ID to carry!

A heartbeat's pause.

"Would you do that?"

Jack, my son. For these few months at fourteen, he's just about my height. Sometimes he wears my Levi's, which hang on his boy's body without panache, without panache just yet, because at fourteen he's androgynous. Except for his dark coloring, he could almost be me. That tender skin with hardly a hint of down on lip and jaw, those huge dark-lashed brown eyes that at this moment are fixed on me.

"Would you do that?"

And some perverse imp stirs in me—can it be done? Could he, could I get away with it?

Hairpieces and wigs are fashionable in 1974, and I've got a wig with a lot of swirling dark curls I comb down over his forehead. I touch up his skin with a little foundation and add an outdated pair of my glasses that have ugly big gunmetal frames with rhine-stones in the corners. My prescription for nearsightedness is so strong that Jack can't see a thing through the glasses, although his eyes swim out at me. Now what. His Levi's and boots, either sex could be wearing those. I give him my beige car coat and scarf to wear, and, because a fourteen-year-old boy's hands are a dead giveaway, I add a pair of my gloves.

There. He looks passable to me. With the horrible glasses and the wig, he looks positively middle-aged and dowdy.

Just then his younger sister, Elizabeth, arrives from wherever she's been and takes a startled look before she recognizes him. She points her finger at him and bursts into laughter.

"Shut up! Just shut up!" he yells.

I cannot possibly send this kid downtown to the movie the-ater by himself. I've already seen the movie, I don't want to sit through it again, but I'm going to have to go along in case he's arrested for—what—impersonating a female? I'm not sure if it's against the law or not, but I know what I'm in for.

After I have driven downtown and parked across from the movie theater, Jack gropes his way, blind behind those glasses, while I purchase two adult tickets at the window. In the lobby, the moonlighting assistant principal of the high school takes the tickets from me, tears them in half, and hands back the stubs without a glance at my companion. Just as well, I think, that Jack can't see him. Only after we've settled into our seats in the darkened theater does Jack whip off the glasses. We've done it, we've pulled it off!

Even though I saw *Last Tango in Paris* twice in 1974, I find that I remember little about the film, either the explicitness that caused all the furor back then, or its claims to artistry. The famous scene with Marlon Brando and Maria Schneider and the butter is the only one I can recall in any detail, and that's because of the butter jokes it engendered: there was a time when you couldn't ask someone to pass the butter at a dinner party without setting off a round of nudgings and guffaws. I do remember how Jack tore off the wig the moment we were safely back in the car that night, and I know I tried to discuss some of the cinematography and the themes of the film with him—*growing older is a crime!* But I don't suppose I brought up the butter scene, and God knows what Jack made of it, sitting there beside his mother in the dark, wearing her clothing and watching sodomy.

The escapade itself became a story to be told over and over, how I'd dressed Jack in my clothes and smuggled him right past the assistant principal of the high school to see *Last Tango in Paris*. At the time I supposed Jack enjoyed the story as much as I did, the story of how he got to be the only kid in town to see the film every other kid wanted to see.

Then Jack's father came back to town for a visit. We had been divorced for a year. He heard the *Last Tango* story and smiled at me (pityingly, I thought).

"I was careful not to let him know what I really thought, so I wouldn't spoil his pleasure in that stunt," he said.

I don't think I answered, but I did cherish his remark in my secret store of evidence that he was trying to turn the children against me. Outwardly, he and I both insisted we were being civilized; we both denied our bitter dance. Of course we weren't circling each other for any signs of thin skin or open sores! Of course we weren't as shifty eyed as two fighting cocks intent on the blood thrust! Any barb had to be disguised as the most casual of observations. What do you mean, I was belittling you to the kids? I was just making sure they got the real story!

FLASHBACK TO 1959. In accordance with the practice of the day, I had had my pubic hair shaved and been given an enema and then left alone in a dimly lit and echoing room. My husband had hovered, anxiously, for a while, but the nurses had sent him home—*nothing's going to happen for several hours*—and, truth to tell, I was relieved to be rid of him, because he had kept asking me questions. How long is it going to take? Yes, but how long do you *think* it's going to take? It was costing me such an effort to respond, I kept wishing he could just be there and be quiet, but it wasn't in his nature.

Yes, but how long do you think it *might* take?

I don't know. I don't *know*!

It took all night, as it turned out. I lay uncomfortably on my back, as I had been ordered by the nurses, stared at the ceiling light, and listened to the sounds of the hospital filtering from the corridor. I cried during the contractions, but otherwise I was bored, bored as time dragged. Next time, I promised myself, I'll bring a book (and I did).

When I awoke from the anesthesia I found myself alone in a hospital room. Eventually I was brought an eight-and-a-half-pound baby boy with the deep furrows left by the forceps on both sides of his tiny skull. I remember being relieved that my labor was over, but distressed with the changes in my body (loose abdomen, stubbled mons, vaginal bleeding heavy enough to soak the heaviest of sanitary pads), and absent any surge of maternal love for the baby in my arms or wonder at the "miracle of birth."

I did the best I could, people are likely to say. I've said it, trying to convince myself, and I've played the *what if* game, over and over. What if I had been willing to measure my life by the ironing of socks and underwear. What if I hadn't gone to graduate school, what if I hadn't divorced Jack's father, what if I were a better person. The *what if* game dances like those ancient apples, forever tempting, forever vanishing in air. Who can ever know *what if*?

I don't know if I did the best I could. I am who I am, and I did what I did.

But I'm not the only one who plays *why* and *what if*. From time to time I will meet another woman, often a visiting writer, and she and I will talk in the way two professional women meeting for the first time will begin with pleasantries and veer closer to the personal: the reading, the likes and dislikes, the family. Sometimes there is chitchat about daughters. Then she says, *son*, and the word is like a stone. *We don't speak*, she says. *I don't speak about him.*

So I HAD A little boy to wash and feed and lug around with me. As an infant he was colicky and cried a lot, but I became fond of him. I was all he could count on, after all, and I rocked him and walked him and nursed him until my nipples chapped and bled. Also, I protected him from his father, who was having his first extended experience with a baby and wasn't liking it. Here was this squalling, puking thing he hadn't asked for, making the nights hideous and claiming all his wife's attention after it had ruined her figure! The first thing he'd done after the baby was born was to turn her sideways to him so he could check, and sure enough, her stomach bulged. And now her boobies leaked milk! It was enough to make him sick. Wouldn't it be funny if he came up behind the squalling, bawling brat and whacked him over the head with a book?

Yes. It happened. The little boy, perhaps eighteen months old, sat crying on the floor. His mother was doing what—homework, perhaps? And perhaps she had appealed to her young husband to see what Jack was crying about, to entertain him for her for just a little while, wouldn't he please? Yes, perhaps she said these things, perhaps she was doing her homework instead of comforting her baby herself, but she doesn't remember, because the memory is like all memories that are not narrated into after-the-fact stories; it is a snapshot, and in the snapshot she looks up to see the book coming down—*thwack!*—on the little boy's head, and the stunned, startled look on his face, and the smirk on her husband's face, as though he has just done something particularly clever.

What happened next? She thinks she remembers flying out of her chair, snatching up the baby, screaming—screaming what? She doesn't know, because that is the end of a snapshot that was never narrated into a story of any kind. Never told at all. Not to anyone. Never until now.

Jack survived. He grew into an affectionate little boy. I remember the texture of his skin, the weight of him in my arms. He loved to be read aloud to, and I dug out my childhood favorites and got reacquainted with the Beatrix Potter characters and Thornton W. Burgess's little caddies of the Green Forest and the Green Meadow: Peter Rabbit, Reddy Fox, Jimmy Skunk.

Soon enough we had moved on to *Just-So Stories*, the very same green-covered book I had discovered on a long-ago summer afternoon.

Could it have been the summer I discovered I could read fluently? Opening *Just-So Stories* and touching pages worn to velvet takes me back to a day I followed my mother and my rancher grandmother along a two-track dirt road to visit the old ranch house where it sagged among its weeds and hollyhocks and overgrown purple phlox with its back to the creek. While my mother and grandmother rooted around for canning jars or whatever else they'd stored in the deserted house, I explored dusty rooms that smelled of mice and crumbling plaster and disuse and found the old staircase that led to what once were bedrooms, where sunlight fell through dirty glass in patches across ancient floorboards strewn with mice droppings, and there I came across a box of junk that contained a book with a faded green cover.

My father's name was written—*still* is written inside the book, *Albert Hogeland, Jr*, in my rancher grandmother's handwriting. A relic of his childhood.

Jack and I finished *Just-So Stories* and moved on to *The Yearling*. Then *White Fang*. One afternoon we had reached the last chapter of *Smoky: The Story of a Cow Horse*, where Clint finds poor old broken-down Smoky after years and years and rescues him from the wagon and the whip, and Jack began to cry. At the sight of his tears, mine began to flow. There I sat, reading aloud with my face streaming to the little boy cuddled under my arm with his face streaming, when Jack's father came along from wherever he had been, and gasped, "What's wrong?"

The summer Jack was eight, I read aloud the whole of Tolkien's *Lord of the Rings* to him, all three volumes. I am certain of his age, because we were still living in Columbia, Missouri, at that time, in the Shamrock Trailer Court on the edge of a gully choked with undergrowth where Jack and his friends loved to play, and I had the pleasure of hearing another little boy shout, "I'll be Superman!" and Jack shout back, "I'll be Aragorn!" When he was eighteen he would give me a copy of Tolkien's *The Silmarillion* as a birthday gift. But in 1967, the gully below the trailer court was infested with poison ivy, and Jack would come home with oozing rashes on his face and arms and legs and the certain knowledge that he would get a thrashing from his father for playing where he had been told not to. That summer, as we read our way with Sam and Frodo up the slopes of the Mountain of Doom, he leaned his infected cheek against my bare arm, and in a few hours I, too, wore an oval patch of poison ivy rash.

He loved music. Later he said that he used to sit with his head pressed against the stereo to listen to the Bach and Mozart I was playing in those days, but I don't remember that. I do remember signing him up for piano lessons, and trying to get him to practice, and finally giving up and letting him quit. And then being surprised when he said he wanted a guitar. No point in buying him an expensive one, I thought, and so he learned on a cheap piece of junk with strings that wouldn't stay in tune, until finally I realized that the guitar was no passing fancy for him and bought him the most expensive one I could afford.

"What's your son majoring in?" a friend asked, when Jack had been in college a couple of years.

"Guitar."

"My God," she said. "I didn't know there was such a major."

Trivial memories. One summer—he was twenty, home from college—he saw a used clarinet advertised for sale in the local paper. Why not? He brought the clarinet home, spread its sections out on the living room floor, puzzled out how to assemble it. Put the reed to his mouth and blew.

Not a sound.

"What do you think I ought to do?" he asked me.

I knew nothing about clarinets. "Blow harder?"

He took a mighty breath and blew into the clarinet, and it emitted a horrific squawk of pain and protest just as one of my cats happened by, and the cat nearly jumped out of its skin as it spun and fled. I laughed, Jack shook his head, and that was pretty much the beginning and the end of the clarinet, which lived in a bureau drawer for some years, until I packed up the house and moved, and I don't know what became of it.

He got his degree in music. Guitar. Then gave up the guitar, but that was much later, after he had stopped speaking to me.

SICK WITH DESIRE. Between divorcing my children's father and meeting the man who would be my second husband, I burned with desire. Burned. As I write, I am startled to realize that that period of my life lasted just three years, almost to the day. How could it have been so short a time when the scorch marks have lasted so long? And over so little—the two or three brief affairs, fumbling and clumsy, that ended in tears and depression that wouldn't lift.

Sick with desire. My body was my enemy. For years I had bludgeoned it into submission: marrying young and bearing the two babies, having sex with my husband when he insisted on it and completing a PhD in literature and, God knows, ironing the socks and underwear. But now my body had the upper hand, and it burned, and my adolescent son lived in a house that throbbed and trembled with his mother's thwarted sexual energy.

But when Jack was fifteen, Bob Blew breezed into our lives with his gifts and his grin and his energy and his private airplane.

It was Bob who flew Jack and me to another city to pick out the expensive guitar, and it was Bob who bought cowboy boots for Jack and a saddle for Elizabeth, who hated him.

She was thirteen. "Promise me you'll never get married again," she said.

I laughed. "I'll promise never to get married if you'll promise never to get married," I said.

"Mother!" she screamed. "That's not fair! You've had your shot!"

Then she threatened me. "If you won't break up with him, I'll go and live with my father."

She did leave. She went to live with her father and her young stepmother in another city, and I was anguished. What kind of a mother, her own daughter, etc., and a daughter who had been the child I had wanted, the pregnancy I had welcomed. She'll be back, friends told me, but I didn't believe them, and I grieved. But I didn't give up Bob for her. In the meantime Jack was the good son who went to school and got a weekend job and got along with Bob, seemed in fact to *like* Bob—what am I missing here?

I was in love with Bob, I was in love with his exuberance, and I was in love with his body. Fifteen and more years after his death, the memory of his body is so sharp that I shudder with it; my skin tingles when I think of that fine-textured skin that no longer touches mine, that soft blond body hair, the power of the muscles and the underlying bone structure of the college halfback he once had been. Flesh of my flesh—those are not just words; and so, for a few years, the teenaged boy lived in a house that was replete and luxurious with sexual pleasure.

Memories break in pieces, scatter. Which have reassembled themselves in the wrong order, which have been lost? The dates that I can string together like beads—weddings, birthdays, deaths—can't account for the fragments.

But here's one date I'm certain of: Rachel, daughter of my marriage to Bob, is exactly ten months old, which means it is the twenty-ninth of July, 1983, and the leaves of the weeping birch outside the window sway green and gold from silver branches and shiver the light in patches across the kitchen floor. Rachel is a blue-eyed baby who looks like her father. The firm little body in my arms. I set her on her feet. Jack—if Rachel is ten months old, Jack must be twenty-four and home for the summer—Jack holds out his arms from the other side of the kitchen and coaxes the baby. *Come on, you can do it!*—and she staggers, her first steps, eight, nine, ten, eleven steps until, crowing in triumph, she falls into his arms.

Bob had been diagnosed with pulmonary fibrosis, a progressive and incurable disease of the lungs, a few months before Rachel's birth. By that golden July day in the kitchen when Rachel took her first steps, he was losing weight along with his lung capacity. He was so short of breath that he could not walk from the kitchen door to his truck without stopping to rest. Short of temper, short of comprehension, dozing by day and wakeful by night, he refused medication, denied he was ill, and withdrew into a fantastic shadowland as he lay on the sofa and chain-smoked the cigarettes he could not give up.

So he was disintegrating, yes. And it must have been shortly after Rachel took those triumphant first steps in the kitchen that she woke from her nap with a fever of 106 degrees.

I tried to rouse Bob—"We've got to take her to the emergency room."

"A-aa-ah," he said, and turned over on the sofa and pulled a pillow over his head. *A-aa-ah* was a guttural, dismissive sound in his throat that meant I was overreacting, that I should get over whatever was agitating me and leave him alone. I had gotten so used to *a-aa-ah* that I had stopped paying attention to it, but began gathering such of Rachel's things I would need for the short drive up to the hospital.

Elizabeth followed me. As everyone had predicted, she had moved back home after a short stay with her father and step-mother. She had seemed to get over her antagonism with Bob, and now she was attending Northern Montana College. "Would you like me to drive you?"

"It would be good if somebody would," I agreed, and so she got her car keys and I got in the passenger seat with Rachel radiating heat like a small furnace. At the emergency room we met the pediatrician, and he was reassuring and spoke of antibiotics and fluids but advised hospitalizing her for a day or two, and next thing I was in an upper-floor room watching Rachel pull herself up on the bars to explore a strange crib while a nurse went through the complicated procedure of preparing a baby girl for a urine sample. Rachel was what there was in the world, and those were the dimensions of her world, about eight by ten feet, because nothing existed beyond the hot lights and odors of disinfectant in the room that held my baby in her crib.

At one point Elizabeth reappeared. "Jack and Bob have had a big fight," she said, and I shook my head and said I didn't want to hear about it. It wasn't until Bob appeared, fully awake and as concerned as any father, that I remembered I had a husband and grown children.

"Wanted you to hear it from me before you hear it from him," he said. "He jumped all over my case, said I didn't care enough. I wasn't taking that shit off him, I shoved him into the couch—"

And I shook my head; I must have shaken my head; I must have shaken off all ability to remember what else he said. All I remember is that Bob and I hovered over Rachel's crib, that we left the hospital only for food and a change of clothes and came back to hover until she and the antibiotics fought off whatever had sent her temperature spiking and we could take her home.

PULMONARY FIBROSIS IS A terrible illness in which a net of fibroids gradually constricts the lungs. As body tissues are starved of oxygen, they begin to deteriorate. Muscles shrink, the brain fails to comprehend. Sometimes the disease can be managed by a course of steroids, but Bob refused to believe his diagnosis and refused treatment. By the time Rachel was two, he was exhibiting symptoms similar to bipolar disorder. For weeks he would be so depressed that he could not dress or eat but would collapse on the sofa in his underwear, smoking his endless cigarettes; then, without warning, he would be infused with manic energy and a conviction that he was about to pull off some get-rich-quick scheme. When he had run through everything he owned, he sold his rifles, wheedled money from friends, and disappeared in the direction of his native Kansas to start life all over again as an oil field developer.

It was months before we heard from him. When he finally called, Rachel was old enough to talk to him on the telephone—"Daddy? When are you coming home? I'll be a good girl if you'll just come home."

Our home was not a place anyone would choose to be. It vibrated with my anxiety: where was Bob, and what would he do next? What new venture, what debts, what looming financial disaster? What would I, should I, do next? Both my older children fled—Jack after his fight with Bob, Elizabeth shortly after. They had transferred to Montana State University in Bozeman, three hundred miles southwest of Havre; they were silent and offended by me. Why? I asked myself, when I had time to wonder. What had I done to them, what had I left undone.

But I had little time to wonder. I had a small child to support, and I had a job that was becoming more and more tenuous as the small college where I had taught for so long was racked by budget shortfalls. During a time as splintered and unstable as light falling through leaves, a time in which I filed for divorce and Bob returned from Kansas, wild-eyed and skeletal and gasping for breath, to try to coax or harass or threaten me into staying married to him, until finally he slapped my face with all the impotent fury remaining to him and I watched red and purple shards of light spin through my head with the force of that slap, sometime during those years my son and I must have spoken for the last time.

Were Jack's and my last words some inconsequential patter, *have you fed the cat, have you seen the paper*, on the afternoon before Rachel woke from her nap with a fever? I remember that Jack came back to play a guitar concert in Havre with three of his friends, and we must have spoken then, but did the concert take place before the episode of the fever and the fight, or was it earlier?

You remember the first step your child takes, someone told me, and you remember the first story you ever read to your child. And the first word your child speaks. But you don't remember the last, because you don't know it is going to be the last.

The summer before Rachel turned five, I finished out my contract with the college in Havre, and my sister and brother-in-law helped me move, by dead of night, away from my deranged and dying husband to another state, to Idaho, to start another life.

In the meantime Elizabeth and Jack graduated from Montana State University. Elizabeth married and moved with her husband to southern Idaho, and soon Jack followed her and got a job at the school where she was teaching. While neither was in touch with me, I knew they were seeing a lot of their father, and in my paranoia I imagined their conversations about me.

She gets herself into these situations.

I could have told her so. But she always thinks she knows what she's doing, and then look what happens to her.

She never should have married Bob Blew. She should have known better.

She ruined her own life.

I feel sorry for her, really. But she did it to herself. Nobody's fault but her own.

Serves her right.

"He warned me to be careful," Elizabeth reported of her father, when she told him she was divorcing her husband and getting back in touch with me.

"Why?"

"He and Jack believe that you are evil and manipulative."

IN THE TWENTY-FIVE YEARS since my son and I last spoke, I have made another life for myself. I am no longer the frightened girl who did not want to be pregnant, nor am I the woman who was sick with desire (as we age, the hormones recede and leave us in peace, says a friend, and in part I believe her). I live within a circle of daughters. Elizabeth lives near me with her second husband and their children, and Misty, the foster daughter I took in when she was fifteen, also lives nearby with her husband and children. I have seen Rachel through a psychotic episode and a lengthy hospitalization, and now she has a child of her own. All this since I have spoken to my son.

Occasionally I have seen my son, at a distance. Playing the guitar (which eventually he took up again) at Elizabeth's first wedding. Sitting on the far side of the room at Elizabeth's graduation from veterinary school. When I heard that he was getting married, I sent, via Elizabeth, one of my handmade quilts in hopes that it would offer peace. Elizabeth didn't want to be put in the middle, but she took the quilt to his wedding, then reported back that he had received it with anger. On the first Christmas after his marriage, I sent presents to his small stepsons and got word back, through those tortuous family channels, that the presents were unwelcome.

So far there's no awakening gargoyle, but I am aware of another kind of silence, the silence of what I do not hear.

We're never going to have children!

The story never told, of the smack of the book on the baby's head.

Aa-aa-ah!

AT THE MONTANA FESTIVAL of the Book in Missoula a few years ago, I gave a reading and spoke afterward with a little line of people. A young woman with lovely long blonde hair waited until everyone else had drifted away, then approached me.

"I'm your daughter-in-law," she said.

Once I recovered my voice, she and I talked for some time. She wanted to be a writer, had been working on a novel and a memoir. She had told Jack she was coming to Missoula to meet me, and he had said all right, and maybe my mother can help you, but don't try to spring a reunion on me.

Since then I have been in touch with my daughter-in-law, and I have talked with her several times, and I have read some of her work. She is a talented writer. But I do not believe she knows, any more than I, the reason for my son's silence.

MY MOTHER DIED in February of 2004, three months short of her ninety-first birthday. Her grandchildren, including Jack and Elizabeth and Rachel, served as her pallbearers. I found the funeral service difficult. My mother and I had never been close, and she had found my divorcing my first husband, whom she had loved, particularly difficult to bear. Now my first husband sat somewhere behind me in the hundred-year-old Presbyterian church, and Rachel sat in front of me, worrying that she would make some mistake in her pallbearer duties. The minister read the list of my mother's descendents, and I smiled as my niece's two-year-old son looked up, his attention momentarily caught by the sound of his own name. At last the service was over, and we all drove out to the cemetery, and Rachel helped to bear her grandmother to her grave without stumbling, which had been her biggest fear.

At the reception, I talked with second and third cousins I had grown up with, but hadn't seen in years, and I heard again and again the mantra I had heard at family funerals all my life: pity it has to be an occasion like this to get us together. Turning from one of these conversations, I found myself briefly meeting the eyes of a slim, dark-haired, dark-mustached man whom I recognized only as he winced and fled.

He was in his midforties, after all, and I knew him no better than he knew the woman I had become.

5

Nowadays anyone in search of me at eleven o'clock at night will be likely to find me, as I was on the night of May 19, 2007, reading in bed in a circle of lamplight with my window open to the dark whispers of cottonwoods barely stirring their shadows over my roof. My bedroom is my quiet place, carpeted and wallpapered, where I unwind with a book and a glass of whiskey from whatever the day held. The oversized bed is the one Bob and I shared, but I have slept alone for many years, now, and I have come to treasure my solitude.

What was I reading on the night of May 19, 2007? I don't remember, probably a detective novel. Probably I had been listening to music, perhaps a recording of Handel's viola sonatas I'm fond of, but that night the disc must have spun to a close, because the night was absolutely still, hardly even a breeze to rustle the young cottonwood leaves, when through my open window I heard a burst of gunfire, thirty or forty rounds being fired somewhere to the west.

I closed my book and tried to focus on what I had just heard. Thought I'd heard. Gunfire. But it couldn't be, I told myself. Someone would have to be shooting up the town with a semi-automatic rifle to set off so many rounds. No, it must have been a string of firecrackers. But it hadn't sounded like firecrackers, it sounded like gunfire. And with that thought, I heard another thirty or forty rounds from the direction of downtown.

The town of Moscow, home of the University of Idaho where I now teach, nestles in the rolling hills of Idaho's Palouse country, where rural roads and fields of wheat stretch to meet low, unassuming mountains. Its population is just a little over twenty thousand. By the third week of May, with finals over and most of the university students gone home for the summer, the town feels quiet; empty, even. Not a town where anyone expects to hear gunfire in the night. I listened for another minute or two and repeated to myself I had heard firecrackers. As if in rebuttal came a third burst, thirty or forty rounds.

If it was gunfire I heard—and surely I had heard over a hundred rounds—somebody was seriously shooting up the place, and I felt an urge I knew was irrational, to get dressed and get in my car, drive down my tree-lined residential street, turn west under the widely spaced streetlights that illuminate a playing field and a couple of silent churches, and follow Sixth Street along six or seven blocks of darkened houses to the downtown, where I would help out. It would be no more than a five-minute drive. But of course I did no such thing. I heard no more gunfire—or firecrackers, surely I'd heard firecrackers—and eventually I put aside my book, turned off the light, and went to sleep.

The bedside phone woke me. The glowing numerals of the alarm clock read three a.m. as I groped for the receiver. My daughter Rachel was on the other end of the line, calling on her cell phone from her bedroom in the basement of my house. She was crying.

"Chris just called," she said. Chris was her ex-boyfriend, the father of her infant daughter. "He told me to take Cali out of her crib and take her in bed with me. He said people are shooting up the town. First they shot up the Safeway store, and now they're riding around in cars, shooting at people."

"*What?*"

"I already locked all our doors and windows," said Rachel.

BY THE TIME I heard those first bursts of gunfire, a woman named Crystal already lay dead in what was later described in the papers as a run-down brown house east of town. I knew the area, because Rachel had had a friend in junior high school who lived out there, and I occasionally drove her home, but I never knew which was Crystal's place. I kept picturing it as a mobile home, perhaps because there are many in that neighborhood. Or maybe, with a skip of association, I was thinking of the trailer I lived in when I was in graduate school at the University of Missouri in Columbia, in a place called Shamrock Trailer Court.

That trailer wasn't really too bad. It was ten feet wide, with a corridor that ran all the way past the cubbyholes where our children slept and opened into our bedroom at the back. For the first year or two we lived in Columbia, the trailer wasn't air-conditioned and the summer heat was oppressive beyond anything we Montana kids had ever experienced. I studied for my PhD qualifying exams that first summer, sitting in the bathtub full of tepid water.

By the final year of my PhD program, we had installed a

window air conditioner in the front room, but I was spending a lot of time alone in that back bedroom. The walls were paneled in imitation birch, and the closets and drawers were built in. On the headless double bed I had a white candlewick bedspread I'd gotten with Green Stamps, but certainly not the high-thread-count sheets and down pillows I've collected in the years since.

During that final year in graduate school, I was exhausted all the time. Any time I had a free hour, I would drive home from campus after teaching a class or sitting through a seminar, park the car in the graveled space next to the trailer, stumble through the door and down the narrow corridor, and collapse on the bed. My husband would be at his teaching job, Jack and Elizabeth at their school or at the after-school babysitter's (Rachel, of course, not yet dreamed of). I had the house to myself. I didn't know what was the matter with me; I only knew I couldn't drop down on that bed fast enough.

All too soon the alarm clock would buzz, and I would have to drag myself up and comb my hair and drive back to campus to whichever class I had to teach or attend.

During the evenings I plodded around, cooking dinner and getting the children fed and bathed and read to. Jack was a second-grader that last year we lived in the trailer in Columbia, and Elizabeth was a kindergartner, and they had had five years of having their suppers served around stacks of library books or xeroxed articles or piles of typescript. My husband wasn't home to witness the afternoon naps I snatched, but he was annoyed by my unwillingness to enjoy his favorite situation comedies with him on the black-and-white television set we had splurged on and by my lack of interest in sex.

"Hey! We're missing *Flipper*! Come on, Mary, you gotta watch this!"

Sign of the times: Ann Landers chiming in with advice for a

woman who complained that her husband was always after her to watch television programs she disliked. *Give his programs a chance, honey. It'll be good for you and your husband to sit down together, and who knows? You may eventually start to enjoy his programs.*

It is hard for me to imagine how either my husband or I thought our marriage could continue without an explosion from one or the other of us. But I buried my resentments and dreamed of the time I would have finished my degree and we both would have good jobs and we would be happy, and he may have dreamed of a time when I would have finished my degree and gotten academe out of my system and we would be happy.

I had come to college with a notion of majoring in drama and becoming an actress, a secret carefully kept from my family. My husband was just as opposed to the damn-fool actress idea as my parents would have been, if they had known about it, and he gave me no peace until I switched my major to English, which was also his major. Secondary education majors in English were sought after in those days. Little high schools all over Montana were competing for English teachers, and after graduation he would get a job as a high school English teacher, somewhere in prime hunting and fishing country, and I would get a job at a nearby school, and we would have two salaries, and we would be happy.

I didn't object to switching to English. I wasn't making much headway in the drama program, but I loved the Latin classes I had begun for no particular reason, my English professors were praising my writing, and my stories were being published in the student magazine, *Venture*. What I didn't get around to was signing up for the teacher education classes I would need for a secondary teaching certificate. In retrospect I think it was the book-lined shelves in my professors' offices that tipped the balance, because it seemed to me that life could hold nothing better than a book-lined office and a class in Shakespeare to teach. One literature class led to another, just as one baby led to another and next thing I had Jack and Elizabeth and a graduate teaching assistantship that would lead to a master's degree, and I was looking around for a PhD program that would have me.

My husband hadn't caught on until too late that I wasn't going to qualify for a job in the school nearby his high school in prime fishing and hunting territory. He worried about the creative writing classes I kept signing up for. He thought every story I wrote was about him. He thought I was exposing our private life for the world to read (or at least for the handful of people who read *Venture*). He thought I was betraying him, and he stormed and he stomped around until I resigned myself to academic, not creative, writing. The world, I told myself with more than a touch of self-righteousness, didn't need another second-rate fiction writer. And so it happened that we hauled our trailer house from Missoula, Montana, down to Columbia, Missouri, and set it up in the Shamrock Trailer Court so I could begin teaching as an instructor of English and studying in the PhD program at the University of Missouri.

He hadn't asked for the life he was living. He hadn't wanted to move from Montana to Missouri. Once, on the road during the move, he had turned to me with tears in his eyes and cried, "I want to go *home*!"

Was I sympathetic? No.

But he got a teaching job at Jefferson Junior High School in Columbia and worked on and off at a master's degree in history while I started the PhD program in English. Secretly I was terrified at the size of the University of Missouri campus, which at that time enrolled some thirty thousand students and employed eighty instructors to teach freshman English and other service courses. The instructors worked and met their students in cubicles with glass partitions, where I felt so exposed that I sometimes walked down to the women's restroom and sat in a stall until I got myself back together. Gradually, though, I learned my way around campus, and I figured out where to park and which of my classes were scheduled in buildings so far apart that I would have to run to get from one batch of freshmen on time to teach the next.

NOBODY SHOT UP THE Safeway store in Moscow on the night of May 19, 2007. There were no gangs riding in cars around Moscow, shooting at people. Those were only a couple of the wilder rumors that traveled around town in the aftermath of the shooting that did take place, but the reality was bad enough.

Crystal's husband had begun the evening at another tavern, where he bought drinks for a friend who had just turned twenty-one, and, by all accounts, seemed to be in a pretty good mood considering he was on probation for trying to strangle a girlfriend and was likely facing jail time. Crystal, who had taken him back after the episode with the girlfriend, was at home, probably in bed. Sometime around ten, her husband left the tavern—no, he wasn't drunk, insisted the witnesses—and drove the five miles home, where he kept the semiautomatic rifles that had had locks placed on them after he told a court-appointed mental health professional that he might commit suicide and take a lot of individuals with him.

Just joking, he added.

"YOU WERE ASKED WHAT it was like to go through graduate school with two small children, and what came to your mind was shooting up the town?" said a writer friend.

Something like that.

Nowadays I read in *The Chronicle of Higher Education* about academic women who have to choose between the tenure track and the mommy track, and when I'm asked how I got through graduate school with small children, my only answer is that I don't know. I don't remember. I remember the knot in my stomach. I remember the awful feeling that I was slipping behind, that I would never catch up, never get the freshman English papers graded, never finish reading the books for my Middle English seminar, never finish writing the paper comparing *Beowulf* translations.

Willoughby Johnson, who directed the freshman composition program at the University of Missouri, called all of us first-year instructors together from time to time to urge us to use our common sense (his favorite term) in assigning essay topics and to return graded essays promptly. Other than that, we were pretty much on our own, although Willoughby, who looked and sounded a bit like Charles Laughton with a mid-Missouri accent, would dispense advice when asked about attendance problems or plagiarism problems, always with the admonition to use our common sense. Some years later the chairman of a department where I'd applied for a job remarked that my letter of recommendation from Willoughby was the only one he'd ever read that complimented the candidate on her common sense.

Because he chose all the English instructors, Willoughby had become a de facto one-man admission committee to the department's PhD program, subject, I suppose, only to the PhD qualifying examination. We all supported ourselves on our instructors' salaries. And Willoughby, although he rumbled and scolded, looked out for us from behind the windows of his office where he watched our comings and goings.

"This may not be the smartest composition department in the world," I once heard him growl, "but it's sure the hell the best looking."

"Nobody ever wants to leave here," one of the older instructors told me. "It's like a womb."

I taught four sections of freshman English every semester, feeling like a tape recording of myself by the end of a day, until eventually I was entrusted with survey classes in English literature. Also I took two classes every semester toward my PhD, until the semester I established the residency requirement by teaching two classes and taking four classes. It took me five years to get to the dissertation stage. I was distressed at my slow pace.

And yes, times were different then. No university day care center, no day care at all for children under the age of three. Finding and keeping a decent babysitter was always a nightmare, always a system on the verge of disintegration. The logistics of one car, my husband dropping me off and picking me up, or the other way around, and always the trip back and forth to the babysitter's. Groceries, laundry, every task planned in advance. I remember screaming at my husband to turn down the TV and lend a hand, even though we both knew that housework and childcare were a woman's responsibility. I remember we maintained a fiction that he was being incredibly generous to allow me to attend graduate school—as though the choice had been his to make.

I remember Jack and Elizabeth hopscotching down the long corridor in the trailer where I had laid out pages of my dissertation (cut and paste was a literal process in those days, with scissors and tape) to sort out and reorganize.

I remember my professor of medieval literature, from whom I had taken several seminars, scribbling on the last paper I wrote for him during my very last semester, *I've been puzzled about your performance. You are taking shortcuts, you aren't working up to your ability.*

And yet I also remember sitting with my book in the shade

of the trailer house in Missoula while toddler Elizabeth tried to remember which gap in the picket fence was wide enough for her to squeeze through. Occasional tires on gravel, murmuring voices of the neighbor women who had given up asking me to drink coffee with them. The book wasn't one I should have been reading, it was an old detective novel from the Missoula Public Library I was stealing time for. *Gaudy Night*, by Dorothy Sayers. I had never heard of Dorothy Sayers, never imagined an academic world like the one she was describing, of Oxford towers and Bach choirs and a college staffed by women dons who valued scholarship above compassion. As I read on, I was beginning to live within those pages, walking across quadrangles I had never seen, entering the stone hallways, listening to the discussions of moral responsibility that are the backbone of Sayers's novel. In retrospect I think I was turned by *Gaudy Night*. Spoiled by it, some might say.

UNLIKE ME, CRYSTAL apparently never battled depression. People who knew her describe her as sunny, cheerful, although they also thought she seemed worried.

Crystal had the key to the locks on his guns. Apparently he woke her; the police later said that there had been a struggle, after which he cut the locks off his guns and killed her with a single shot to the head.

With his semiautomatics and his rounds of ammunition, he drove back to town, past my quiet and darkened neighborhood, and turned on Sixth Street, the same street I drive to teach at the university. Halfway along Sixth Street he turned into the parking lot at the county courthouse, took out his rifles, and fired the first burst, the thirty or so rounds that sounded all the way across town and made me look up from my book, into the sheriff's dispatch office. The young women dispatchers on the night shift were, of course, terrified, and ran downstairs and hid in the jail.

The first officer to answer the alarm was a highly respected police sergeant. Crystal's husband shot him dead. He shot and wounded the deputy who tried to pull the sergeant to safety. Then he shot and wounded a college student who had heard the racket, strapped on his own handgun, and ridden up on a bicycle to help out. Then, in probably the second or third burst of gunfire I heard, he fired at random into the various sheriff's vehicles and emergency vehicles parked behind the courthouse. The damage was later estimated in the hundreds of thousands of dollars.

There was a silence. Tree leaves, their edges whitened by streetlights, hung over the courthouse parking lot. Shattered glass on the pavement reflected back the light. Crystal's husband must have looked around, thinking what to do next. He must have known he was cornered. Officers at great risk to themselves had used police cars as shields while they recovered the dead and wounded, and SWAT teams from all over Idaho were on the way. Crystal's husband ran across the street and entered the Presbyterian Church. Here he encountered the sexton, who slept in the basement of the church and had come upstairs to see what was going on. Crystal's husband killed the sexton, a man he probably was acquainted with. Then he climbed up the bell tower, giving rise to another set of rumors about a sniper in a church tower.

～

Three smallish black loose-leaf notebooks have been sitting on a shelf in my office for many years. I took one down the other day, shook dust off it, and opened it at random. Typed in the slightly off-kilter elite font of the portable Underwood I was using in those days are my class notes from my graduate seminars. I see that on September 15, 1966, I was thinking a lot about the relationship between Dryden and Swift, which was "tenuous." By September 20 of that year I'd moved on to the sources for a life of Swift, which begin with an autobiographical fragment, containing several errors and inconsistencies, in which Swift refers to himself in the third person.

It occurs to me that the black notebooks are diaries of sorts. I can read from day to day what I was studying in the Swift seminar, what I was reading in seminars on the Age of Reason or the Age of Dryden. Apparently I was taking notes by hand during class periods, then typing up my handwritten notes on the old Underwood and filing them in neat categories in the notebooks. *Synopses. Critical Articles. Class notes.*

I flip ahead. On October 27, I'd written a note to myself: *Be able to characterize Isaac Bickerstaff.* On December 1, I'm concerned with Book I, Chapter 6, of Gulliver's Travels. *Children need not have obligations toward their parents. The principle of children being educated by the state is common to Utopian literature.*

I remember an afternoon when I was by God going to make some progress on my dissertation research, and I had no baby-sitter, so I took Elizabeth with me to the university library. She was five, and I had bought her a book of her favorite Beverly Hillbillies paper dolls to occupy her. High in the dim stacks I found a quiet table where I could spread out my papers, and I got Elizabeth settled on the floor next to me with her paper dolls. Then I absorbed myself in whatever I was tracking down about Ben Jonson and forgot about her. That total concentration on the printed page is a form of time travel in which the present is negated, sounds fade, and centuries dissolve between one paragraph and the next. I never even realized that Elizabeth had vanished until I looked up from my article and saw one of the library's uniformed security guards bending over me.

"Is she yours?" he asked. He was an enormous man, middle-aged, leading Elizabeth by the hand. Elizabeth looked a little scared but also pleased by so much attention.

"Thank you," I managed. "Where did you find her?"

He had a wonderful rich laugh. "Three floors down."

As an adult, Elizabeth remembers her rescue as one more childhood anecdote. "I wanted to explore. I'd go down some stairs, walk between the stacks of books, down another stairs—"

"How did he know where to find me?"

"Oh, that was interesting. He asked me what kind of tile was on the floor where I'd been playing, and of course I'd been down on the floor with my paper dolls, so I could describe the tile exactly. Then he knew just where I'd been."

Still. Anything could have happened to her. And whose fault would that have been? Not Ben Jonson's.

THE POLICE AND THE SWAT teams waited until nearly dawn, when they heard a single shot. They found Crystal's husband slumped and dead in the bell tower, a semiautomatic rifle between his knees.

Frightened people near the courthouse had taken shelter as best they could. One of my friends told how she and her husband crawled upstairs on their hands and knees in the dark, careful to keep their heads below window level. Another woman and her daughter, across the street from the shooting, spent the rest on the night flattened on the floor. Several of my graduate students, who had been celebrating the end of spring semester at a local tavern a few blocks from the courthouse, barred the door and stayed trapped and incommunicado until morning.

Television news crews had hurried to Moscow. After CNN reported that SWAT teams had cornered the gunman in the church tower, phone calls rang in from worried friends and relatives.

I got an e-mail from a friend in upper New York State: *Are you all right?? What's going on??*

Crystal had worked as a janitor at that county courthouse. Coworkers described her as a pleasant but private person. They worried about her unexplained bruises. One of her friends, however, told reporters, "This was not about domestic violence! Crystal would be furious if she knew people thought it was about domestic violence! It was about her husband! It was about his dark demons! All Crystal wanted was to help him!"

ASIDE FROM MY DEPRESSION, which I didn't know I had, our years in Missouri weren't too bad. My husband's teaching schedule at Jefferson Junior High School was demanding, and he couldn't get away to check up on me, the way he had checked up on me between his classes at the University of Montana. He didn't know my students at the University of Missouri, so he didn't worry about which boys were visiting me in my office, and why, and he didn't have to worry about my fiction, which I'd stopped writing.

My academic papers didn't bother him. What angered him was my loss of interest in sex. Whether it was my workload or my new prescription for birth control pills that was exhausting me, I just wanted him to climb on top of me and pump away and get it over with. Maybe those female dons in Dorothy Sayers's *Gaudy Night* had it right when they assumed that women scholars had to choose between marriage and motherhood or a life of the mind, which of course would be a celibate life. Maybe celibacy would be just fine, at least for now. I was living for the future, when I would have my PhD and he would have his MA and we would both have teaching jobs in the same city, and we would be happy, if in the meantime I could just get some rest. If he would just get it over with so I could get up and go to the bathroom and come back to bed and get some sleep.

"You *never* want to!"

And yet—celibacy be damned—at a time when I flinched at my husband's touch, I was slipping more and more often into a serial daydream of romance and vague eroticism. I daydreamed as I walked (or ran) between my freshman English classes, between student appointments in my office cubicle, over stove and sink and the routines of getting small children to bed, adding tiny increments to the narrative I was weaving from glimpses of television or chance glances from students into a parallel world that was pleasant and full of possibilities and never ending until, from time to time, the daydream did end, and I would crash and sleep. And sleep.

WHAT DOES HE DREAM? Of how, once upon a time, he was promised a different life? That he would wear the pants in the family, as his father always said he would, and that his wife would be attuned to his wishes and otherwise, as his father always cautioned his mother, tend to her knitting? The first time in their marriage that she refused to leave her homework and—do what?—she doesn't remember—write a letter to his mother, perhaps, or type up his term paper when he told her to—he slammed out of the apartment, leaped into his car, and tore out of the parking lot on squealing tires.

What could he do, eventually, but turn around and drive home again? What could he do but persist, insist, keep after her, try to break through her wall of concentration?

She curls on a bed in the darkened room. What has she been dreaming? A night sky. Clouds drift past a moon that is reflected in water. There's a beach, perhaps. Walking toward her is a man, a faceless man, or a man with a face borrowed from some movie or perhaps some classroom. Where's her husband? Erased from the page—or dead—

Just joking!
Depression, they say, is anger turned inward.

IF I COULD JUST stay awake long enough to finish my dissertation.

The dissertation had to be typed on expensive bond paper, with footnotes and carbon copies. I was still using that same old Underwood manual typewriter my parents had bought me when I was a sophomore in high school, but I longed for an electric typewriter, which at that time was the state-of-the-art word-processing technology. The Selectric I had my eye on cost a hundred dollars, which was beyond my reach, until I happened to notice an advertisement for a fiction-writing contest on one of the bulletin boards in the liberal arts building at the university. The first prize was a hundred dollars. I went home and wrote a story called "Lambing Out" over the weekend, entered it in the contest, and won the hundred dollars.

The faculty advisor to the student literary magazine stopped me after the Hawthorne seminar I was taking with him. "It's an impressive piece," he said. "If you can write like that, you ought to keep writing."

The advisor's words didn't necessarily bring about the end of my marriage, but they charged through me like electricity.

"*I* oughta knock out a few short stories."

"*I* oughta be the one to use the electric typewriter, because I'm a worse typer than you are."

"My friend read your story and wanted to know what really happened, and I didn't know what to tell him."

"What are we going to call ourselves? Mister and Doctor Clearman?"

At a time when the women's magazines were full of advice on how to minister to a husband's ego, could I take a hint?

No.

Too bad if you have to drop out of college, but the important thing is to get him through.

In future years I would discover women in classes I was teaching who were deliberately failing tests, lest they shame their husbands. I would cringe at my husband's parting shot—"You'd trample anybody to get what you want!"—but I knew he was right, at least in the sense that I had gone after a PhD as though it were a Holy Grail, that I had cobbled childcare around classes and meals around seminar papers, that my mind was on Old English strong verbs and the ablative absolute, and that I had gone back to writing fiction with a kind of dumb compulsion that I couldn't seem to stop, no matter whom I hurt—

"Who'd you hurt?" demanded the same writer friend who'd teased me about comparing childcare and graduate school with shooting up the town. "Your kids turned out okay, didn't they?"

—and when cornered, I lashed out, if not with a rifle, and then turned the blame on myself.

"He was troubled," Crystal told one of her friends. The friend agreed; Crystal's husband had been troubled since his youth. There were dark places within him; there were compulsions he failed to fight; there were demons. No question, he needed help, but where to get it? The system failed him, Crystal's friends told reporters after the night of May 19, 2007. He had nowhere to go. To help him, there was only Crystal, who kept the key to the locks on his semiautomatic rifles and slept at night with her own loaded handgun under her pillow to ward off his demons.

My story touches his only at the edges. My demons, those otherworldly lady dons of Dorothy Sayers's *Gaudy Night*, have been more benign than his. My tower is a wallpapered bedroom with down pillows and music and a book in a circle of lamplight. And yet I know a thing or two about compulsion.

6

AFTER LIVING FOR FIVE years among the soft hills and lush greenery of central Missouri, then spending another year in rainy green Bellevue with its towering office buildings and its ink fringes of evergreens, Jack and Elizabeth were astonished during that first drive north to Havre in the late summer of 1969.

"Big Sandy?" exclaimed Jack, as the highway took us through the dusty main street of that little town, thirty miles south of Havre, which once was a center for the open-range cattle out-fits, and now is a place where elderly wheat ranchers come to retire and the young people move away. "They ought to call it *Little* Sandy!"

Even today, after the hundred or so miles from Great Falls on Highway 87, the newcomer who drives into Havre is likely to feel the jolt of a mirage taking on shape and form: after so many miles of nothing but sky and sagebrush, here is this town of dusty cottonwoods and willows and irrigated lawns.

"People live here?" a member of a Chicago dance troupe, come to perform at the state college, once asked, incredulously.

Yes! We live here! And don't think for one minute that we'd rather live in your crime-ridden, congested, stinking Chicago! This is a friendly town where our kids can grow up safely and our neighbors will always offer a helping hand. We take care of our own here! We're doing just fine!

On the bluff above the town, facing into the wind, the campus of Northern Montana College lifts a modest assortment of classroom buildings and dormitories toward unobstructed sky. People in Havre are proud of Northern, which stands as another example of their pluck and self-reliance. Also, Northern is a campus where decent, conservative parents believe their children will be safe and sheltered from city temptations or from the radical ideas to which they might be exposed at, say, the University of Montana in Missoula.

A dark side of any isolated, self-contained community is how deeply it may fear outsiders. A particularly ugly incident during the summer of 1970 had fueled the fears of people all over Montana, when the headless, armless, legless body of a young man was pulled out of the Yellowstone River, near Livingston. Eventually the body was identified and the killers traced to a pair of hitchhikers who, by that time, had returned to California. Apparently they had murdered the young man for his car, but also for a grizzlier reason: when apprehended, one of the hitchhikers told police, "I've got a problem, I'm a cannibal," as he pulled a handful of human bones from his pocket and added, "These aren't chicken bones."

Californians! Hippies! Manson-style murderers! Flames and dark dancing figures, chants and blasphemies and slogans written on walls in blood!

The rumors that festered in and around Havre that fall might have been amusing if they had not led to such serious consequences. According to one popular story, hordes of hippies were camping in a public park a few miles to the east, getting ready to invade the town. As evidence, a woman wrote to the editor of the *Havre Daily News* that she had counted 130 hippies getting on school buses in Big Sandy. (Maybe she had seen the Indian fire crews from the Rocky Boy Reservation on their way to fight forest fires, suggested a local wag.) However, fears were beginning to focus on two young men, one of them a black man, who had come from Philadelphia, of all outlandish places, to visit a local girl. The young men were shaggy haired, they wore the disreputable clothing that young people even in Montana in 1970 were wearing, and they were disturbingly *other*. When the young black man was seen downtown in broad daylight with his arm around a white girl, community simmering came to a boil, and rumors went from preposterous to disturbingly plausible.

Was it possible, for instance, that a group of Havre businessmen—names were named, faces pointed out—actually had climbed a butte overlooking the town and burned a cross? *Oh! Yes! I was there! I watched them*, insisted a college student. *A friend of mine filmed it with a home movie camera, got all their faces.*

What certainly was true was that things had gone too far. The young men from Philadelphia had received death threats. But at that point, a respected Havre attorney called publicly for a return to reason. The two young Philadelphia men, he announced, were welcome to move into his home with him and his family and stay as long as it took for them to feel safe.

The attorney's willingness to speak out was, apparently, enough. If rumors of hippies or fear of out-of-towners hadn't dissipated entirely, at least they were no longer overt, and there was no more talk of cross burning.

THE FACULTY AT Northern Montana College—the arts and letters faculty, at least—tended to keep themselves apart from the townspeople and to affect an amused disdain for their rumors. In truth, they were not a part of the town, although some of them had taught at Northern for twenty years or more. Then too, they had their own rumors to worry about.

Times were changing in academe in the 1970s, even at remote little state colleges like Northern. Everyone had read of the student protest movements on campuses in faraway places like Berkeley and Boston, or watched the jerky black and white footage of sit-down strikes and marches on the evening news, and while no one really believed that boys and girls from Highline towns and ranches were likely to start wearing beads and feathers or join radical societies or take over the president's office, the reports stimulated a disturbing thrill, like an electrical charge over a great distance. When, at a fall faculty meeting, a young professor of history whose office was located in the squat tower above Cowan Hall announced that he was requisitioning a length of rope to run out a window and let himself down in the event that students tried to hold him hostage, the laughter was nervous.

Among the faculty was a feeling that not only were their students changing in ways they could not have predicted, so were the circumstances of their own lives. Northern Montana College had been staffed, during the 1950s and '60s, by recruiting seasoned teachers from high schools around the state. To be appointed at the college level was considered a reward for their years of service. No one thought of requiring them to hold doctoral degrees; a master's degree was all the education anyone would ever want or need. Unless you aspired to an administrative position, why waste years on the tedium and expense of writing a dissertation? There was such a thing as being *too* educated. The belief was widely held that, along with high academic achievement, came a lack of practicality and common sense. What wasn't wanted on an unpretentious campus like Northern was a pack of educated fools.

But now the professors at Northern were being told of new accreditation standards that required terminal academic degrees in appropriate fields, and these same seasoned professors were being presented with young colleagues who could write *PhD* after their names but who had never taught in high school, who knew so little and thought they knew so much.

To add to their unease, they were seeing women being hired, and not just as nursing faculty or as faculty in the two-year secretarial program. In spite of certain deeply held beliefs that women were unfit for teaching college-level English courses, a second woman had just been hired in the English department to join the giggly ex–high school teacher who oversaw the teaching certification program. The new woman had a face like porcelain and looked young enough to be a student herself, but icily unapproachable, as though she feared that someone else's smile or greeting might shatter her surface. Something wrong there, but she had a PhD, so what else was to be said?

THE LONG-TIME CHAIRMAN of the English department, George Craig, had had to beat the bushes of Montana to staff his sections. Like their colleagues in other academic departments, most of the seven professors then teaching English had been lured out of one high school or another, although young Mr. Thackeray told how the chairman had driven out to the wheatfield where he was operating a combine and persuaded him to accept a teaching position instead of returning to law school in the fall.

By the early 1970s, however, it was becoming obvious that no longer was there a shortage of qualified candidates willing to live and teach at such a remote and windblown campus but, at least in the fields of arts and letters, there was a surfeit of would-be professors looking desperately for a job, any job.

But George Craig had resigned and taken another job, far away, after losing one of the fierce internecine wars that occasionally raged through the college, and the dean had appointed as his replacement a fiery little potbellied man who held a PhD degree from Harvard and who was so deeply resentful of authority that he started battling with the dean the day he arrived on campus. True to his egalitarian principles, the new chairman had reorganized the English department as a co-op, shaken up the curriculum, and refused to evaluate the faculty. Now he was trying to hire a new young professor, and the dean for some reason was dragging his feet.

It was 1971 by now, times had changed, and hiring was done through advertising and screening by a committee. The professors in the English department had supposed they would be looking for someone with a master's degree and high school teaching experience, but no, said the dean. They had to find somebody with a PhD, and so they settled down to read the tidal wave of applications that flooded into their offices. From these applications they selected a man from California whom I will call Paul Blevins.

"I should be the one to greet him," insisted the chairman, when the on-campus interview was finally arranged. The dean, for some reason, had taken a dislike to the California man from what he read in his paperwork, which enraged the chairman to the point of wanting to hire him, sight unseen.

No, said the dean, there had to be a campus interview.

All right, reported the chairman through gritted teeth to the gathered faculty. We'll play his little game. So the invitation was made to Paul Blevins, and the flight into the one-strip local airport arranged. The chairman would meet him and see him to his hotel room. Once he had had a chance to rest, there would be a dinner party to give the rest of the faculty a chance to get acquainted with him.

That Paul Blevins came from California was both impressive and frightening. That he also had a PhD made everybody wonder why a man so well qualified really wanted to join them. Would he be *happy* here, they asked each other doubtfully. Would he *fit in*. But they had picked him out, and the dean finally had given them a go-ahead, and now they were anxious to get a look at him.

The young woman with the face like porcelain about to shatter was assigned to pick up Paul Blevins at his hotel and drive him to the dinner party. Her husband reluctantly parked at the curb on First Street and waited while she ran in to fetch Paul Blevins; he hated all college faculty get-togethers, but he had no choice. He had to go along and keep an eye on his wife. While they both were in graduate school, he had been able to think of ways to keep her home—there were Jack and Elizabeth to care for, after all—but since they had moved to Havre and the children were older, she was becoming more and more independent, and now his anger was blossoming, and also his suspicions. He knew she was naïve, too naïve even to know when a pass was being made at her, but other people weren't naïve. They would believe the worst. His vocabulary failed him when he tried to explain to her what other people were thinking about her. She was shacking up. Sleeping around. Having tawdry affairs.

"Tawdry?" she said.

"Yes, and if you want to know what tawdry is, think of a color. Brass!"

There goes the notorious Dr. Clearman, he imagined other people

97

were saying as they pointed her out on the street, *and her poor damned fool of a husband.*

The young woman, knowing herself on a knife-edge of civility that must last her and her husband through the evening, hurried through the lobby with its comfortable drone of black-and-white television and shabby chairs full of the shabbier old men who lodged in the old hotel. She had stayed in this same hotel three years ago, for her own interview, and it seemed to her that nothing had changed: same old men, same blurred television footage of faraway warfare. There would be worn chenille spreads on the beds upstairs, and tiny octagonal tiles on the floors of the bathrooms, where the sounds of conversations and flushing water from other rooms would be carried through the pipes, and where, at one or two or three in the morning, the faraway crash of freight cars coupling in the rail yards to the north would remind the sleepless guest that life continued elsewhere. She had lain awake the night of her interview, knowing that she was going to accept this job if it was offered to her, knowing that living in this town was going to change her, never guessing how much.

Now she climbed two flights of stairs and rapped on the door that was Paul Blevins's. For long moments no one answered, and she was just beginning to wonder whether she had made some mistake, wrong room number perhaps, when the door opened, and there stood a tall and robust man with a head of springy dark hair and a face so white that her first thought was that he must be in great pain.

"Dr. Blevins?" she faltered, feeling somehow that she had intruded.

He passed a hand over his face, as though hearing his name had intensified the pain.

"Yes," he said, "oh, yes." When he turned to reach for his coat, she saw that he was carrying a bottle of beer.

I WAS THAT YOUNG woman, as much as anyone is the person she was forty years ago. What can I say for myself? That I was so innocent of the ways of the world that I didn't recognize a drunk when I saw one?

That, although I had an uneasy feeling that something was seriously the matter with Paul Blevins, I lacked the self-confidence to say so?

And yet, when I look back on that sorry episode, what strikes me is not just my lack of judgment, but the lack of judgment shown by nearly everyone who eventually was drawn into the Paul Blevins affair. It is as though, in the convergence of a certain set of circumstances—the iceberg, the ship—instincts more primitive than reason and judgment rise screaming to the surface as though they never had been submerged. Perhaps we can count ourselves fortunate if there is one, like the attorney who put out the flames of the great Havre hippie scare, who not only keeps his or her head but reminds the rest of us to keep ours.

To UNDERSTAND THE Paul Blevins affair, consider the size and isolation of the town and campus. The population of Havre in the 1970s was around eight thousand. The college, with about a hundred faculty and administrators and fewer than fifteen hundred students, lay nearly three hundred miles to the north of the University of Montana, over narrow blacktopped highways that often were treacherous with winter ice and blizzards. To live at such distance from the rest of the world, at a time when cable television and public radio had not yet reached the Highline and the Internet was undreamed of, was to begin to believe that Havre and its campus was the only world that was.

For the older faculty, the college was an extension of the high schools in which they had taught most of their lives, and they felt lucky to be there. On the other hand, the younger, university-trained faculty, chafing at their circumstances, saw the college as a concept to be realized. The college-as-concept explained the radical curriculum revision the new English department chairman, with his Harvard PhD, had undertaken, and also some of his other innovations, such as rounding up a band of unemployed recent BA graduates, appointing them graduate assistants, and assigning them sections of freshman composition. He was apoplectic with rage when the dean, hearing of this program through his spies, fired all the graduate assistants and reassigned the composition sections to the professors. "You don't have a graduate program, so you can't have graduate assistants, and besides, there's no money to pay them," the dean pointed out. "Yes, but we *should* have!" raged the chairman.

The college-as-concept added its fuel to the battles among the Northern faculty and its administrators. Perhaps as a side effect of a no-exit world, grudges were never forgotten and slights never forgiven. Faculty offices buzzed with plots, rumors, and counterplots, all at the deepest level of seriousness, and yet—again, perhaps because all the plots were ongoing, all the rumors constantly metastasizing into new rumors—none of it was life threatening. There were no cease-fires, but also there were no consequences.

That would change.

The fall semester of 1971 began, as it always did, in the wheat dust and sunlight of late September. Cottonwood trees shaded the many-paned windows of Cowan Hall, with its echoing stairs and its warren of faculty offices at the south end of the second floor, and the students came sunburned and healthy from working harvest. These early days of the semester were as benign as though winter would never blast those lush leaves or rattle sleet against the windows, although in fact the first snowfall could silence the campus and town within a few weeks. The chairman of the English department called the first meeting of the fall, and everyone gathered in the dappled light of one of the big classrooms.

There at the meeting was handsome young Mr. Thackeray, who taught philosophy, and there was suave, toupeed Mr. Lisenby, who taught public speaking, and plump, chuckling Mr. Keller, puffing on his pipe, who taught British literature and could recite the plots of every Victorian novel ever written to anyone he could corner at a faculty party. There was Miss Erickson, who was working at getting rid of her giggle, and there was nervous, red-haired Mr. Neisius, who was supposed to have finished his doctorate the previous summer but hadn't. There I was, self-absorbed and frozen, and there was Dr. Paul Blevins. He was one of us, now. None of us saw any significance in the dean's hiring him on a one-year contract.

Later, as the semester wore on and the cottonwoods outside Cowan Hall turned briefly golden and then thrashed their way into sleet-whipped, subzero winter, we would all learn more about Paul Blevins and, for example, the magniloquence of his memo writing. He could turn a sentence or two requesting summer teaching into three or four pages of irony and hyperbole, he could object to some detail of campus governance with reams of satire embellished with the darkest imagery. But at that first department meeting, everyone was hopeful and curious, and many were the glances stolen at him as he sat in our semicircle, expansive in his suit and tie. His headache seemed to be gone, his deep laugh rolled out at unexpected moments, and he gleamed with an inner amusement that told us he knew a thing or two we didn't. All the while our little chairman beamed upon him, proud as a new papa.

While the men in the department seemed to see the chairman as a Quixote, flailing at the academic windmills of intellectual poverty on the one hand and parsimony on the other, I disliked him with an intensity that grew over the years I knew him. For him, women did not exist in academe. It was his duty, as he saw it, to fight for his colleagues and protect them from the dean, but of course his colleagues were men. Miss Erickson and I were—what. Adjuncts, perhaps. Useful takers of notes and instructors of freshman composition. My objections to my class assignments, or to my being overlooked for sought-after summer classes, were likely to be met with an absent frown, or—if pressed in department meeting—a startled titter. *Changing her mind is a woman's privilege*, he was fond of saying. Or, rolling his eyes, he would ask rhetorically, *What do women want?*

Writing about the man after all these years, I find myself wondering if I have invented him. Surely no such caricature could have existed. He's a figment of my imagination, an eater of my sins, a marionette that I've jerked through the decades in his shiny green suit and soiled necktie. I'm embarrassed to be writing about him, *whining* about him—and yet I close my eyes and there he is, nervously licking his lips with a shred of tobacco stuck to his tongue, although his only role at the moment is a supporting one to the explosion of Paul Blevins that winter.

I might have paid more attention to the talk that almost immediately began to swirl around Paul Blevins if it had not been for the misery of my marriage. Because I had accepted the position at Northern, my husband had given up the job in Bellevue, Washington, which he liked, to come and teach at Havre High School. He hated Havre, and he hated the gossip, and he hated the transformation of his wife into *that young woman in the English department*. He felt exposed, felt himself the butt of unpleasant speculation.

"There are other jobs," he kept telling me.

"No, there aren't. Don't you remember how long it took me to find this one?"

I had finished graduate school along with a thousand other young PhDs who were competing for too few positions in the liberal arts, and the job at Northern had seemed to me the last job in the world. I was certain that, if I gave in to my husband and resigned, I would never get another.

He would listen to my explanation, but in a few days he would come back to it. "There are other jobs."

Gossip always swirled on campus, and often it was vicious. What was said about me was that I required my students to hump me in my office, on my desk. What was said about Paul Blevins was that his wife was very young, which was true. That he had had an affair with her while she was in high school and he was her teacher, which had caused him to be divorced by his first wife and fired from his job, which might or might not have been true. That he and the very young wife and their baby son had moved into one of the cottages provided by the college for first-year faculty and covered all the windows with bookshelves and books so they could live in the dark like moles, which could have been true, but what did it signify?

There never was a source for these stories, which were told in the passive voice. *They were seen. He was seen.* If one believed the gossip, we all fornicated and frolicked in some shadowy state that existed simultaneously with our dull daylight drudgery, as though we were a department of doppelgangers. No wonder my husband snarled and tried to see through shadows.

One evening that fall, Paul Blevins showed up in the basement of Cowan Hall, where I was directing the college play. I glanced up and saw him grinning and beckoning from the double doors that opened into the theater. Wondering what on earth, I left my playbook and went out into the corridor to see what he wanted. Whatever it was, he was full of it; he was dancing on his toes, barely able to contain what he was about to import.

"They know all about you," he said, and he laughed, a long exultant skein of laughter that unwound itself down the echoing dark corridor and faded into the land of the doppelgangers.

"*What?*"

"Dr. Crowley and the postmaster. They know all about you."

I stared at him. Dr. Crowley was the president of the college. The postmaster lived up the street from my house. His youngest son was my son's age.

"It's a conspiracy. They're keeping track of the letters you've written to apply for other jobs. They're opening your letters to see what you're saying. I used to work in a post office," he explained, "so I know how they arrange these things."

What struck me, even in the moment, was how absolutely convincing he was. Whether it was the force of his personality, his energy, his massive body as he bent to confide the details of the plot he had uncovered, I was ready to believe him. Utterly. But I didn't believe him, because I had written no letters of application. There were no letters to open, no letters to conspire over.

I don't remember what else he said. I suppose I went back to play practice. I suppose Paul Blevins took himself off, laughing to himself and dancing up the stairs to the double plate-glass doors that reflected him in a black sheen before he broke the illusion and disappeared in the direction of the parking lot. And if, thinking over his behavior, I had an uneasy feeling that something ought to be done, I didn't act on it. After all, what could I have done? Carried the tale to the department chairman?

It wasn't that much wilder a tale than some of the suspicions that buzzed up and down the corridors. Or so I told myself.

I did write in my journal that night, *Paul Blevins is crazy*.

I was writing fiction again, after a hiatus of years. Trying to write fiction. My husband was certain he was the secret subject of all my stories. He would stand over me and my typewriter, cocking his head as casually as though it were the most natural thing in the world for him to be reading the words as I wrote them.

"I see this time you've killed me off," he remarked, sadly, when one character turned out to be a widow.

"I'm not writing about you. Go away."

"Oh, yes you are. Why do you want to hang on to this job? There are other jobs."

"Go away, I'm trying to write."

But he was on the attack now. Driven to distraction by rumors and shaken by the shift in our marriage, he tried to force us back to what we had been before my job—*the job!*—and he used the sharpest weapon he could find. "I want to get this situation settled, once and for all! You're thinking about having an affair, aren't you."

"No, I'm not! Why do you think that?"

"You're not the type that could handle an affair. You'd have a breakdown."

And so on.

Years later I learned that seven-year-old Elizabeth had lain awake, listening to our raised voices and sobbing softly to herself, small sufferer from the misery of marriage. "It always ended with you crying," she said. It was true; I always ended up in tears and my husband half-triumphant, half-abashed. He was terrified of losing me, he knew he was losing me, but he didn't know why, and all he could think to do was to insist and storm and accuse until he had reduced me to a sodden bundle of tears, which was not what he wanted at all.

What did I want? I knew my husband was right; the job wasn't even a good job, the college library was inadequate for scholarly research, and the teaching load was four classes a semester, most of them basic writing classes. I knew I was hurting him and hurting our children by my stubbornness. Why did I hang on to the job, why did I insist on writing fiction when my writing caused him so much distress? It was my fault, I knew it was my fault, and surely it wasn't worth it. And yet, just as I had plodded through graduate school through protests and recriminations, I kept writing and I plodded back to Cowan Hall every day, locked and frozen inside myself and hoping not to give more offense than I was already giving.

Rumors aside, Cowan Hall was a safe place where secretaries typed in the administrative offices downstairs and the heat registers puffed away. Snow might swirl against those high single-paned windows, the wind might rattle against the glass, and conspiracy theories might abound, but Cowan Hall had withstood worse, and it stood foursquare and solid under its squat tower, and I had my mailbox in the alcove next to the campus switchboard, and I had my small office with my name on the door, and the classrooms next door were filled with boys and girls in mackinaws and cowboy boots and blue jeans who knew as little as I once had, but were willing to learn. The saving grace of Northern was the solid teaching that went on there.

If I give up the job, I'll be at his mercy, I said to myself, without quite allowing myself to know what I meant.

WITH THE WINTER CAME fresh swirls of rumors about our embattled little chairman. He had been the subject of speculation ever since his arrival: how had a man with a PhD from Harvard come to end his career on the Montana prairie? Who did he think he was? Did he have no sense of self-preservation? His quarrels were legendary; he had insulted President Crowley, he had disobeyed the dean, he had picked fights with everyone from the manager of the book store to the cooks in the college food service in his wholehearted belief that, through his own persistence and force of argument, he could transform the practical programs at Northern into a rich liberal arts curriculum. Now came word that he was going to be removed as chairman of the English department. He couldn't be fired, because he had been hired with tenure. But, beginning with the next academic year, he would be just another professor with the rest of us, and someone else would be chairman.

Few events in academe, perhaps in the world, are so catastrophic that the survivors don't begin to speculate on what personal opportunity might open for themselves, and so it must have been with Paul Blevins. On the one hand (so rumor had it), the chairman had gone directly from the dean's office to Paul Blevins's office and wakened his fears by saying, "They got me, and you're my protégé, so they'll be gunning for you next." On the other hand, the shoes that carried the old chairman from the dean's office to Paul Blevins's office could hardly have picked up another scuff before heads were together, calculating. *Let's see. Since they can't fire him, they won't have an open position. They can't hire from outside. The dean will have to look inside, which means one of us will be the new chairman. But which of us?*

Has to be someone with a PhD. Remember those accreditation standards? The chairman of a department has to have the appropriate terminal degree.

Paul Blevins?

THIS, I BELIEVE, is the direction Paul Blevins's thoughts spun. *Could he be so fortunate? But wait! There's Dr. Clearman. She's got a PhD. But they wouldn't, would they? Appoint a woman? —or would they?*

And so he showed up on my doorstep, late one evening. I went to see who could be knocking at such an hour and saw him grinning through the window and holding up his six-pack of beer. My husband took one look at him, gathered up his papers, glared at me, and moved down to the basement to finish grading.

Paul Blevins seated himself at my kitchen table and opened a beer. He had a story to tell, and he was looking forward to telling it, but first he downed his beer. Laughing, pausing to take deep draughts from a fresh beer, gleaming and giggling, he began an involved account of how he had learned that the local homosexuals were plotting to take control of Northern Montana College.

"I called Roger," he said, naming a young unmarried professor of art. "He said, *Hello?* I didn't say a word. I just waited on the line. After awhile he said, *Bill?*"

Paul Blevins exploded into laughter. "Can you believe it? He said, *Bill?*"

I was trying, in my literal-minded way, to understand what was incriminating about saying *Bill*.

"They almost caught me," Paul Blevins was explaining, his breath whistling at his narrow escape. "They had a party and invited me, but I knew enough not to go. Otherwise they would have caught me, too."

I felt as though I was listening to an eerie reprise of his post-master plot, except that this one was less coherent. But in spite of his laughter and his fractured details, a narrative of sorts emerged. I think it emerged. Every story has not only a teller, but a listener, and every story contains not only what was told, but what was heard. It may be that I was too gullible a listener, it may be that I gave to his details a more distinct frame than Paul Blevins ever intended. He was to insist, in the aftermath, that he had been misunderstood. Misunderstood, or perhaps deliberately framed. But as he told his story, I was dazed by the names he listed, all of whom I knew, some of whom apparently were active members of the homosexual ring, some of whom were being blackmailed by the members of the ring, as Paul Blevins himself would have been blackmailed if he had attended the fateful party. Our little chairman was an active member of the ring, of course. *Of course.*

At that time—the winter of 1972—there was little discussion of homosexuality in Havre or on campus, at least that I was aware of. Considering the fervor with which all other sexual activity was speculated on and embellished as the stories developed, in retrospect this lack of interest in gay sex seems surprising. *Gay*—I don't believe I'd heard the word at that time in that context. *Queer*, I'd heard, and always pejorative. I remember that *homosexual*, Paul Blevins's word, didn't seem overly formal to me. I had read James Baldwin's *Giovanni's Room* and I knew people I supposed were gay, and I had heard one or two nasty little rumors that were intended to be hurtful. But I had not a clue why Paul Blevins would think that homosexuals were likely to try to take over a college campus, or why he thought that I would think so.

"I'll need your support," he ended his tale. "They'll have their way on campus unless we stand up to them! We'll be an alliance of a true man and a true woman!"

Eventually, his beer drunk up, he took himself off, and eventually my husband came angrily back upstairs, and we quarreled, of course. Why did he have to go downstairs and leave me alone with a drunk? Well, why did I have to involve myself with drunks? Why, when most of the time he hovered over me, did he go off and leave me alone when I could have used his support? Well, why, when I brought these situations on myself, should he have to get me out of them?

So I never did tell him about the homosexual ring. But it worried me, and the next morning, when I ran into Miss Erickson as I hurried into Cowan Hall on some last-minute errand (I was traveling that day with a group of student actors in a children's play to a nearby town), I blurted out the whole tarradiddle. Miss Erickson's reaction was to laugh, which reassured me. It was a funny story, really. No need to worry further.

And yet, that afternoon, when the principal of the elementary school where my students were performing pulled me aside and said I was wanted on the telephone in his office I was stricken with dread.

It was the dean.

"I don't want to get into the details over the phone," he said, "but I understand one of our faculty has made certain allegations regarding others on our faculty. Is this true?"

I have never been a good liar. "Yes," I whispered.

"Are you willing to confirm what you were told?"

"Yes."

Why? Why didn't I do the decent thing and lie?

"I'll want to talk with you first thing in the morning," he said, and hung up.

My dread was spawned by a deep sense of guilt. This was *my fault*. At the very least, it was going to be construed as my fault, for listening, for *telling*. I crept home, crept around the house that night, crept to campus the next morning for my eight o'clock meeting with the dean.

As I opened the glass door into the suite of administrative offices, I glanced over my shoulder and saw the librarian unlocking the door at the other end of Cowan Hall. He gave me a curious glance. I knew what that meant. *She was seen on her way to the dean's office.*

I had made one phone call the night before. "Did you tell anyone?" I asked Miss Erickson.

"No," she said, puzzled. "Well—" and she named the dean of students. "I happened to run into him right after I talked to you, and I thought the story was so funny that I told him about it. He laughed and laughed."

In fact, the story had struck the dean of students as so funny that he had laughingly asked the academic dean what he planned to do about the homosexual plot. The academic dean had not been amused. Therefore his phone call to me, therefore, therefore.

"He was hired on a one-year contract," said the dean, after he had pried my story from me, "and it won't be renewed. He won't be given a reason. The only person who needs to know is your chairman—he's still the chairman, until the end of the year—and he must be told why one of his faculty members will not have his contract renewed."

"He'll go straight to Paul!"

The dean leaned back in his chair and regarded me. I seem to remember sunlight falling through the window behind him, making hollows of his eyes and patterning the shoulders of the off-the-rack suit all administrators wore in those days. He had been a football coach at a Montana high school before becoming a college administrator, and he was still very lean, with a graying crew cut and a face like a skull under a tight, tanned mask of skin. He would go on to become Montana's commissioner of higher education before he was done. Before he was done. Before he and his wife and adopted son drowned in a sailboat accident. But all that lay in the unforeseeable future, and for now I shook under his gaze and dreaded my own future.

"He'll be warned not to," said the dean. As though that would be that.

That was my morning. I dragged myself through the rest of my day, dragged myself home. I cooked dinner, I suppose. My husband had gone back to the high school to do some work of his own when the telephone rang. I knew, knew as certainly as though I had been writing the script, who was calling.

"Hello," I whispered.

There was a whistling silence on the line, as though over miles and miles.

Finally, "Oh, yes!" sighed Paul Blevins.

I could think of nothing to say.

"I've been hurt," he sighed. "I've been badly hurt, and I'm going to see that others are hurt just as badly before I leave this town."

He waited, but it was as if I had no voice. I was shaking, I could say nothing, and finally, gently, he hung up the phone.

"What? What?" demanded Jack. He and Elizabeth were wild-eyed, sensing my fear.

"There's a bad man," I managed, and then the phone rang again.

It was President Crowley. "Mary, did you get a strange phone call this evening?" he wanted to know.

"Yes," I managed, wondering how on earth he knew.

"We think he's dangerous," said President Crowley. "Mary, is there anywhere you could go for a few days, or a few weeks? Out of town?"

"My parents' ranch," I said. "But my classes!"

"That would be excellent. Don't worry about your classes. Go to the ranch and stay there. Other than that, I don't know what to tell you, except to lock your doors and close your curtains and stay away from the windows."

He hung up. I stared at the phone. If only I knew more. After a minute I dialed his home phone number.

His wife answered. Her voice was pleasant and noncommittal, although campus lore in the aftermath would have it that her husband had called her, given her the same advice he had given me—lock the doors, close the curtains, stay away from the windows—without context, and then he had hung up on her.

"He's not here," she said. "He went up to his office on campus."

The college switchboard would have closed at five. He could call out, but no one could call in. I couldn't think what else to do. I wanted to pack, but both children were crying, so I gathered them up and rocked them until, finally, my husband came home.

"This is all your fault!" he screamed. "My busiest time! And now I've got to drive all night, to get you to the ranch!"

"I'll drive myself!"

"No you won't!"

By this time it was nearly midnight. Our headlights lit the empty street as, with the four of us crammed into the cab of the truck with what clothes I had snatched together, we pulled out of our driveway. A few years later, a student who had been working as a police dispatcher told me that my house had been under surveillance all that night, but I saw no police presence at the time. The town was silent, only a few dim security lights burning in stores. It was a weeknight and even the bars were quiet. All the noise in the world was contained in the cab of the truck with us, as my husband's fear and outrage and bewilderment twisted into diatribe. He had never asked for this flight into the night. He did not deserve the trouble I had caused him. He was up to here with it, he had had all he could take, and it was all my fault. For the three-hour drive through the darkest part of the night, over snowbound highways, my husband's voice ratcheted through my head. He may not have screamed for the entire three hours. It seemed, still seems to me, that he did. Then, in the small hours of the morning, with the children settled into a state closer to stupor than sleep, we had driven through Lewistown, up the winding county road through pine forest, and were pulling up to the pole gate by the snow-covered barn. There was a light burning in the ranch house, a hundred yards on the other side of the gate.

LEWISTOWN, WHERE I WENT to high school, lies in the shelter of several low mountain ranges. The wind is not as fierce as it is on the Highline, and the snow in winter lies deeper. There had been several feet of snow at the ranch that winter, and its white light fell through the windows of the old house. For three weeks Jack and Elizabeth and I lived in stasis, while President Crowley and the dean negotiated with the state board of education to buy out the remainder of Paul Blevins's contract on condition that he leave town. Otherwise, as President Crowley pointed out to me over the long-distance telephone, he would hole up in his cottage and drink and brood, and who knew what he might do.

Rumors on campus had boiled over. My husband, who had turned around in the barnyard at four a.m. and driven back to Havre to teach the next morning, reported over the long-distance telephone that he had had a series of calls from the chairman, begging to know where I had gone. The chairman had conceived the notion that if only Paul Blevins apologized to me, everything would be all right and Paul would have his job back. The chairman was sure everything could be smoothed over. He was telling everyone that I had gone to be with my sick father. No one had to know what I had done. My husband finally slammed down the phone, locked the house, and went to stay with a friend to get away from the incessant ringing.

"He was worried sick about his family. That was why he was so angry," my mother tried to soothe me.

For those three weeks Jack and Elizabeth played upstairs in the old stone ranch house while I read and embroidered and worried about what would happen when we went back to Havre. One day my father took me to town, picked out a pistol for me, and made me practice firing it until he was sure I could shoot straight.

"Mom, are you going to wear that gun on your hip when you go back to class?" asked Jack.

On another day my father hitched one of his teams of horses to a hay sled and took the children and me for a drive across snowbound meadows where sunlight danced on frost crystals, and pine trees cast their blue shadows and occasionally dropped their snowcaps into a world that was otherwise peaceful. Jack and Elizabeth were bundled to their noses, and they got to hold the lines of the horses, and around the haystacks in the high pasture they saw deer that raised their heads at our silent passing and went on eating hay. I thought how it had been my choice to leave this place, a choice nobody understood, and soon I would be going back to Havre, to try to piece together what was left of the semester. President Crowley had called to say that it was safe, that Paul Blevins was gone, but I was desperately afraid that the rest of the faculty would agree with the chairman that I had gotten Paul fired.

ALL THIS TOOK PLACE during the winter of 1972. That spring my husband told me that he was resigning his job at Havre High School and moving back to Missouri. He didn't think he wanted to be married to me. The dean is dead—drowned with his family in a sailboating accident, as I have said—and President Crowley is dead, and so is Mr. Lisenby. I suspect our fiery little ex-chairman is dead, although I lost track of him after he retired. Miss Erickson is retired and living alone, in bad health. I visit her once or twice every year, and when, on my most recent visit, I told her I was writing about Paul Blevins, I was surprised to learn that she did not remember him.

The only person I knew in 1972 who still teaches at Northern is young Mr. Thackeray, no longer young. I ran into him at a writers' conference last summer, and I asked him if he remembered Paul Blevins. He laughed and said he was probably the last person in Havre to see Paul; he'd helped him pack his books and odds and ends out of his faculty cottage and into a U-Haul for his move to—wherever he went. He was never heard from again.

I had returned, that winter, to a campus that was surprisingly calm. When I remarked on that calm to Miss Erickson, she had explained that when the rumors and speculation had reached the point where it seemed as though the English department was about to combust from its own excitement, Mr. Lisenby—suave, toupeed Mr. Lisenby—had gone around to everyone's office and said, in effect, *Pull yourselves together! Get over it! Enough!*

I went down to his office to thank him, but he only smiled.

Mr. Lisenby's wife had received a phone call from Paul Blevins on the night of threats. "Who are you?" Marian Lisenby was said to have said. "You sound like you're drunk. I'm hanging up."

Paul had had a busy night on the phone. Some of his calls were friendly, some were maudlin, and others, to members of his so-called homosexual ring, so threatening that some of the men were frightened nearly to hysteria. But for years I wondered what would have happened if, during his call to me, I had had the poise to have said, as Marian Lisenby did, "Oh, Paul! You're drunk! Come off it!"

As I had with his postmaster conspiracy story, I must have let Paul think I believed his homosexual conspiracy story. I hadn't argued or tried to reason with him, hadn't dismissed him, but had listened and waited for him to go away. Now I wonder if he saw in me a naïve young woman who would believe anything he told her. I wonder if he thought his homosexual conspiracy story would frighten me into supporting him in his bid for the chairmanship.

If that is what he hoped, he was mistaken. The dean, mistrustful of Paul from the beginning, was only too glad of an excuse to be rid of him, and rid of him he was.

The other thing that happened that spring, besides the end of my marriage, was that the dean called me down to his office and offered me the chairmanship of the English department, thus confirming—what?—whose paranoia?—and certainly my sense of guilt.

7

MOST FRIENDSHIPS GROW gradually, and I cannot remember how Trev's and mine began, or even a moment when I might have said to myself, *he is my closest friend*. What I do remember is a moment that could have been any of a thousand moments. It might have been one bar, it might have been another. Trev, as slight as a ten-year-old in his shirt and blue jeans and top hat, sits across the table from me. He's drinking vodka and 7 Up, and I'm drinking a Square Bottle Ditch, which is Canadian Lord Calvert with ice and water. It's wintertime—in Havre, Montana, it's almost always wintertime—and outside in the thirty-below-zero night the streetlights spin with granules of snow that the wind whips against the parked cars and the windowless walls of buildings and the faces of bundled-up people hurrying for the shelter of the Stockman's or the Hackamore or the Jubilee. Inside the bar is sanctuary, a deep dark velvet warmth where the snow can't seep under the doors and the howl of the wind is stilled, and nobody but the barmaids has anything pressing to do. Deep in this safe place, time loses track of itself until one of the barmaids yells, "Last call!" and we realize it is ten to two, and we ask for go-cups for our last round of drinks.

An improbable pair we must have seemed: Trev the dwarf out drinking with the young chair of the English department, that *woman-with-a-PhD*, as she was sometimes pointed out on the streets of Havre in the 1970s. One night when Trev and I had been dancing in the heated crowd on the Three Hundred Club's dance floor and returned breathless to our table (not that either of us could dance, but we could prance and flail with the best of them to *Bad, bad Leroy Brown, baddest man in the whole damn town*), a young man tapped me on the shoulder. "Will you please tell my girlfriend that you're a professor at the college? She doesn't believe me."

I was thirty-two when I took the chairmanship of the English department, and I still looked so young that I often was mistaken for a student. From the beginning, I had felt lonely and uncertain at Northern. I missed being one of many young graduate students, and as a woman I felt conspicuous. Once, asked to a meeting of the graduate faculty—*an assistant professor on the graduate faculty, what were they thinking!*—I froze on the threshold of the conference room when I saw a dozen or so balding men in suits sitting around and waiting for things to start. I couldn't bring myself to walk through the door; I fled down the hall to my own office to hide. Later, of course, when I got acquainted with those same men and learned something about their anxieties, I felt foolish about my fears, but that was, well, later.

Now, after my husband had moved back to Missouri without me, I suspected I was watched and speculated over—*is she still married, or isn't she, and what's her game?*

For his part, Trev said that until third grade he was always one of the biggest kids in his class. It wasn't until he was eight or nine that his dwarfism started to make itself apparent. His parents must have been half-expecting it, because the dwarfism gene ran like a constriction through the males in their family. Uncles, cousins. Trev's older brother was normal—Trev joked that his brother stood six feet three, while he himself stood three feet six—so what were the odds?

I don't know whether his parents looked into medical treatment, hormone therapy, or whatever was available at that time, which would have been the early 1960s, but Trev always said they were the best parents in the world. They loved him, they never pitied him, they always expected just as much of him as they had their older children. By the time he was in his teens he was riding a tractor or combine just like any other Montana Highline farm boy, seeding or summerfallowing or harvesting wheat on the family acreage, although he always used a cushion on the seat of whatever rig he was operating so he could see where he was going.

It was when he came to Havre and enrolled as an English major at Northern that I met Trev. He cut a curious figure in those days. To give himself a bit of extra height, he wore high-heeled boots with the blue jeans and T-shirts that would have fit a child, and somewhere he had acquired the black top hat that gave him the appearance of a character from a fairy tale. His facial features also might have come from a fairy tale as well as his Norwegian emigrant ancestry; along with those sweet blue eyes came a thatch of tousled blond hair and a hooked nose, like a young troll, or perhaps a Viking in miniature.

Students who had known Trev in high school said he had been an ornery little devil, by which they meant something beyond devil-may-care. One of his favorite pastimes, for instance, was hunting rattlesnakes, which abounded in that high dry prairie country. He knew where their dens were, and he smoked them out and then killed them with rocks. Characteristic of that time and place, nobody thought killing rattlesnakes was inhumane or perverse, although they thought Trev was crazy for taking the chances he did. His lack of size must have put him nearly at eye level with some of the coiled and buzzing snakes, and he was bitten so many times he had lost count. Fortunately, one of his older sisters was an emergency room nurse at the local hospital, and after a snakebite, Trev would drop by to get an antivenom shot from her. He showed me one of his scars from a rattlesnake bite: a small round white patch on the web between his thumb and fingers.

If nobody worried about the deaths of rattlesnakes, nobody in the 1970s ever seemed to worry about the heavy drinking that went on in Havre and the other little towns strung up and down the Highline. Local merchants routinely donated kegs of beer for high school parties; at least their kids weren't smoking pot, was what a lot of folks told themselves. At least it was just beer. And for those over twenty-one, the bars in town rocked and rolled until two a.m. every night. How many bars were there in Havre, population a little under ten thousand? Thirty bars? People were always trying to count. They would leave out a bar, or count a bar twice, and there would be an argument.

The classiest of the bars was the Red Lion on the west end of town. Its barmaids wore cutaway red miniskirts over ruffled white panties, and as they hurried back and forth with trays, their legs flashed in the light from the back bar that glittered on the rows of bottles in front of the mirror. In the Red Lion it was possible to order a fancy drink, a Pink Lady or a White Russian, and lean back in deep leather chairs on carpeting so deep that voices were lost in it and thoughts were dissipated into a darkness so lush as to be palpable.

Or if a din was what you were looking for, there was the Three Hundred Club across from the stockyards on the highway east of town. The Three Hundred Club held the weather at bay in a cavernous room where country-western bands nearly drowned out the crash of pins from the attached bowling alley, and the dancing was packed and frenetic on a miniscule dance floor, and everybody drank beer or boilermakers and bawled along to the lyrics, until you couldn't hear yourself think, which was the whole point. *Proud Mary keep on rolling! Meaner than a junkyard dog! Elvi-i-i-ra!*

In between the two ends of town, strung along First Street where a chill wind off the Rocky Mountains blew unobstructed grit and snow into drifts across sidewalks and into alleys, were your choices of bars. There was the Stockman's, where if you asked for a Square Bottle Ditch, you'd get your Canadian Lord Calvert in a glass with water and crushed ice. There was the Oxford, which was a railroaders' bar where a brakeman coming off a shift at nine in the morning could get a beer, and there was the Duck Inn, which was attached to a restaurant where you could get frozen lobster tails and a bottle of red wine to accompany your steak. There was the Hackamore, and there was the Jubilee, and there was the Vets' Club, and there were several more I don't remember the names of. A block to the north off First Street, toward the railroad tracks, were the shabby White Horse and shabbier Gables where the Indians drank Strawberry Hill and Thunderbird and fought with pool cues, and where whites ventured at their peril.

Back of a raw lumber façade on First Street was a bar that

went through several owners but kept its plywood tables and sawdust floors. For a time it was called Danny's, later the Shack. It tended to be a college hangout, and some of my students were there the night a newly hired English teacher at Havre High School achieved brief local fame, or infamy, by getting roaring drunk and delivering a speech in which he damned the town and everybody in it. As a culminating gesture, he yanked out the machete he always carried, God knows why, and attempted to drive it through the table. The problem, as several people later pointed out, was the plywood, which the machete penetrated only to a depth of perhaps an eighth of an inch, where it wobbled before it fell over.

Then, reported the students, a couple of local bankers (what were bankers doing in the Shack?) overpowered him and frog-marched him a block down the street to the police station, where he was charged and booked with—what?—the story begins to fray at this point. Threatening people with a machete? Insulting them? Whatever the charges, the result was that he lost his job and left town.

When my husband was hired to take the machete wielder's place at Havre High School, I had been overjoyed. What had been the machete wielder's ill fortune, or ill-conceived choice, or perhaps his deliberate decision to get out of his contract with a flourish, had turned into our good fortune. We had finally achieved what had seemed to be impossible: we each had a job in the same town.

WHAT WOULD WE HAVE been talking about, Trev and I, with our heads together over our drinks?

Theater, probably.

Theater was the reason Trev had enrolled at Northern Montana College. He never attended any of his other classes; he hung on through special pleading and petitioning, semester after semester, and eventually he flunked out, but in the meantime he spent his nondrinking hours with me and a company of dreamers and druggies and misfits in the rickety little theater in the basement of Cowan Hall.

Theater was what was holding me together.

Within a month of moving back to Missouri, my husband was writing and phoning that he had decided to give me another chance. But we wouldn't be living in Havre. No! He'd already made that decision. He couldn't stand Havre, he couldn't stand my friends. He was pretty sure of getting a teaching job in Helena, Montana, where he'd grown up, where his parents still lived. We would be within easy driving distance of great trout fishing and elk hunting—

I felt suffocated at the very idea. Back in the same town with his parents, with his mother standing over me in the kitchen, trying to make me wear a dress and an apron instead of my blue jeans, insisting that I use the cheap cake mix that didn't call for eggs, lecturing me for spending good money on real vanilla instead of the cheap imitation stuff, demanding that I bring Jack and Elizabeth to her fundamentalist church for services every Sunday. And I would have no job.

What about my job, I asked over the long-distance line.

There are other jobs!

How I hated the chirp in his voice—*there are other jobs!* I knew there weren't, not for me in academe, and I'd worked too long and hard, tried too hard for a professorship to give it up easily. But I was shattered by the separation, all the same. I had been married since I was eighteen, and I didn't know what to do with myself on my own, and I didn't know who I was. *That woman-with-a-PhD.* The anger I had been stifling for all the years I could remember was turning into self-hatred, and a crazy text of voices in my head blamed me over and over for my mistakes:

my marriage and my disappointments, my perverse insistence on pursuing a graduate degree. The truth was that I wished I had never married my husband, I wished never to see or think about him again, and yet I thought about him constantly. I took to heart his accusations: how he had been cheated out of what he had a right to expect of marriage, how my headstrong ways had absolved him of any further obligation toward me, how his unhappiness was all my fault.

Looking back at that anger and self-pity and despair, I ask myself what I would have told that young woman (if I had known her then, I almost write).

Would I have suggested to her, in the language of popular therapy she would not then have been familiar with, that she was internalizing her anger? Urged her to get some counseling?

But there's no clinical psychologist closer than Great Falls, which is 110 miles of single-lane highway from Havre, highway that's often snowpacked and blizzard blown, and for another, I'm a ranch-raised Montana girl who's had it embedded in me from childhood that there's hardly a worse sin than talking about my feelings!

I'm exasperated with that girl; she's as bad as one of my own children the way she stands there and argues with me. What else can I try to tell her? That she's living through a time of social and economic transitions, and that she might as well whistle into the wind as try to reverse them? Yes, pay attention, you silly girl, while I explain that, in a very few years, inflation and rising standards of living are going to make the two-income family the norm. The Working Wife will lay aside her scarlet W, and the expectations of your mother's generation, and your mother-in-law's, will seem quaint.

It isn't just my job. It's my education. My mother and my mother-in-law both believe that my college education has made me unfit for marriage, and I half believe they're right.

Another thing, and trust me on this, a piece of legislation called Affirmative Action is going to mean that girls like you won't routinely be counseled into secretarial jobs. Girls like you won't be ridiculed for their aspirations. First-generation college students like you are going to be given help, not heckling, for raising their heads above their horizons. Furthermore, more women are going to be earning advanced degrees and entering the profession, and you aren't going to feel like such an aberration.

Are you listening to me?

My husband is right when he objects to the way I've been behaving. Buying clothes, for instance. All during college I went without, and now for the first time in my life I've had a little money to spend on myself. I admit it, I like feeling attractive. And I admit, I've gotten in the habit of meeting friends for lunch, or for a drink—a couple of drinks—

So what's the problem? You got married too young, and you felt left out of all the fun, and now you're looking for trouble? Trouble is what you're likely to find, you know.

THAT SUBTERRANEAN little theater in Cowan Hall with its cramped and dusty stage and its creaking wooden seats was my escape. Down in that ill-lit space, with its paucity of ellipsoidals and Fresnel lights, I could lose myself in a make-believe I was perpetuating in more ways than one.

Why did a small college like Northern need a theater program? Especially a small college that was gradually turning away from its traditional emphasis on teacher education and redesigning itself as a vocational-technical institute? Its bachelor of arts degrees were being canceled, its core curriculum pared away. Students majoring in auto-body or diesel or metals increasingly complained. *Why do I have to take a history class when I'm just gonna be a welder?* Their instructors lobbied for further reductions in requirements, while professors in history and literature taught their shrinking classes as they always had and pointed their fingers of blame at the vocational-technical faculty voting bloc, the college administration, the state board of education, and the state legislature. Faculty meetings became forums for jeremiads: *How can we call ourselves a college if we don't offer a foreign language? If we don't require a core curriculum? If we don't require college-level math? We're going to be the laughingstock of the university system!*

Out of earshot, deep as a mole under Cowan Hall, I constructed an alternate reality. All I knew about theater was what I'd picked up while studying Renaissance drama in graduate school, but some of the students had asked me to direct *The Sandbox*, and that led to a production of *Anne of the Thousand Days*. Underground, I studied books on set design that I had borrowed from the library and wondered what in the world Edward Gordon Craig, for example, had been trying to accomplish. Those dark and elongated drawings, all pen-and-ink crosshatching and wispy shadows, offered no guidance to how I might recreate the modernist artistry of Craig's faraway civilization in my remote northern borderland, and so I fell back on common sense, planning a series of levels that would look interesting, make the best of my cramped stage, and fall within the range of my carpentry skills.

I didn't know anything about carpentry, either, but I studied the stairs and supports in my own basement and made notes, and on Saturday mornings Trev and I went to work with whichever students were sober enough not to pound their thumbs or buzz off a hand with a power saw. For tools and lumber and paint we wheedled funds from every available source; we made nuisances of ourselves begging before the board of the Associated Students, we hit up bankers and tavern owners for donations. What we couldn't afford had a way of appearing, anyway.

"Who do you think I am? King Rat?" I heard Trev growl at another student, and I didn't ask what he'd been up to.

On a campus of welders and goat ropers, we were drama freaks. We spent pleasant winter Saturdays in the basement of Cowan Hall, where the heat pipes gurgled, and the scent of fresh-cut lumber rose from our set building, and frozen daylight never penetrated as Trev and I and the others hammered away. One basis of Trev's and my friendship was the ranch-raised Montana kid's figure-it-out-and-do-it outlook that we shared. He and I were serious about work; we both liked a good, clean job, where we could look back and see how far we had come, which in the case of stage carpentry was both a reality and an illusion.

Stage makeup? I got a book out of the library, ordered some supplies from a theater catalog, and practiced on my own face. One afternoon I sat in front of the streaked mirror in one of the stale underground dressing rooms and used gobs of latex to transform myself into a wart-ridden, sagging hag (I was thinking of producing *The Eumenides*). One of the girls wandered in, saw my face in the mirror and screamed, and then, as I turned, she recognized me and screamed again.

Costumes? At least I knew how to sew. Old fur coats from the local Goodwill became robes for *The Lion in Winter*, and the Bishop of Beauvais trailed lawn vestments made of someone's sheer curtains through *St. Joan*. Red taffeta cancan skirts for the chorus line in *Paint Your Wagon*? I could find a way. Imagination was the main thing. To turn Trev, notoriously hard to cast, into a cannibal in the Wild West show for *Annie Get Your Gun* (well, why not a cannibal, when nothing about the show or our performance of it was realistic), we dyed his skin brown, greased his hair and twisted a bone into it, gave him a larger bone to brandish, and he was all set.

Where were teenaged Jack and Elizabeth while I was absorbed

in theater? Much of the time, at least during the school year, they were right there on stage. I have a snapshot of Elizabeth in a dog costume in a children's play, and I remember her skittering on all fours across the stage and wagging her tail. Jack, who had a lovely tenor voice, played the second Von Trapp son, Kurt, in *The Sound of Music*, and the lovelorn young Hero in *A Funny Thing Happened on the Way to the Forum*, and beguiling Matt in *The Fantasticks*.

Were they well enough cared for? I hope so. Were they the center of my life? God, no.

They always seemed to enjoy the theater, but they also loved my parents' ranch, where they spent weeks of their summers riding horseback and training 4-h colts under my father's guidance. He hadn't had the time or energy for such excursions when I was in my teens, but now he put the stockrack on his truck and loaded their colts and drove Jack and Elizabeth to meetings of the Horse 4-h Club and horse-o-ramas and meets. Next thing, he was helping other children with their colts. Next thing, he was the official leader of the Horse 4-h Club. I shook my head, feeling a little envious at such adventure on a ranch that always meant isolation and drudgery to me and a little guilty at my summer's freedom from responsibility.

All the same, several times a year I would load Jack and Elizabeth and their dogs into the MG Midget I was driving in those days and roar through the night on the empty highway across the Fort Belknap Reservation, through the game reserve, and across the Missouri River on what was still known as the New Bridge. No seatbelt laws in those days, hardly any speed limits in Montana. I'd unload the kids and dogs at the ranch and turn around and drive back.

One time, driving through the reservation at about two a.m. I was pulled over by an Indian Police cruiser. I watched in the rearview mirror as the patrolman climbed out of his car and trudged up to the MG. He was a huge man, easily six and a half feet, and he had to bend nearly double to look through the MG's window. What he would have seen was a car full of eyes: the woman driver with two kids and two dogs startled out of sleep and staring back at him. All he said was,

"You were weaving over the center line. I just wanted to make sure you were awake."

Another time I was driving back from the ranch in the middle of the day in the big Ford XL my father had helped me pick out after a student had borrowed the MG and totaled it. For some reason Jack wasn't with us, but Elizabeth was in the back seat. The AIM movement had reached the Fort Belknap reservation, and I knew white women who wouldn't drive across it, but I'd never been worried—

"Yes, but the Indian police are *pulling people over*!"

"Possibly to make sure they're awake when they weave over the center line?"

However, on this afternoon I crested one of those long, low prairie hills and saw, a mile ahead, a car pulled halfway across the highway and several young guys standing around it, on the lookout for traffic. I had heard of such blockades, and that the guys would be looking to collect a toll, and maybe this story was true. I glanced back to warn Elizabeth to lock her doors and saw that she had decided to change clothes and was wearing nothing but her underpants.

By this time we were almost upon the blockade. There was just room to steer the XL, big and heavy as it was, around the Indian guys' car, or there would have been if the Indian guys hadn't been standing there in the middle of the highway, and I reacted without thought and floored the gas pedal.

The XL had had its valves ground, and I must have been going ninety by the time I could see the idea bloom in their faces—*she's not going to stop!*—and, in what must have been split seconds, but felt as though I was watching in slow motion, they dived for the borrow pit. I was miles down the highway before they could climb out again. And ever after, I would wonder, what if I'd killed somebody?

You wouldn't get in these situations if you were home where you belonged. Especially if you were home where my mom could keep an eye on you.

I WAS ALWAYS SURPRISED at how willing, eager even, the rest of the Northern faculty were to be recruited as actors, or at least as technical advisors. I remember an instructor of metals coming down to the stage to oversee some weird contraption of pipes with which I was trying to build a revolving set (and which, during a performance of *Oliver!* creaked and lurched but revolved). Or the professor of music, thundering along on the piano accompaniment to *West Side Story*, briefly taking his hands off the keys to put them over his ears during the pistol shot that felled Tony. Or the professor of history in *Oklahoma!* waving a pitchfork and capering in bib overalls while he sang, *Oh, the farmer and the cowman should be friends!* Or the four professors who donned the red taffeta skirts left over from *Paint Your Wagon* and danced the cancan for the approval of a roaring, clapping audience.

Their enthusiasm for getting dressed up and singing and dancing or carrying a spear in front of an audience was, I thought at the time, an example of a primitive cooperative spirit that, like the magnetism that attracts children to pitch in and help build a snow fort they see in progress, drew otherwise sober and respectable folk into the strange project they saw unfolding under Cowan Hall. I now think I overlooked the sheer appeal of foolery for professors who led daytime lives where curriculum changes heralded the end of the world. *We're going to be the laughingstock of the university system!* Who wouldn't want to escape underground to sing and dance? Who wouldn't welcome laughter and applause?

After rehearsals, the other professors would go home to their families, but the students and I would gather at somebody's off-campus digs, and we would drink and play pinochle until dawn. Or else we would head for one of the bars, promising ourselves *just one or two*, and then drink until last call. Havre had no open container law at that time, and at two a.m. we'd stagger out with our last drinks in go-cups and drive out to the all-night restaurant for breakfast. As a young college instructor, I had been warned against trying to make friends with my students. *You may feel close in age to your students*, I remember a senior professor lecturing us novices, *and you may think they're enjoying your company and laughing at your jokes. But they aren't. They're laughing at you.* And maybe they were, but in a town where the adults were organized two-by-two into married couples, where was I to turn for friends?

The drinking. Nobody thought anything about it. I remember the student we called the Peacock, swaying on his feet and laughing down at Trev—"If size has anything to do with how much you can hold, why aren't you drunker than I am?"

The Peacock was well over six feet tall, merry-eyed and flamboyant. He had grown up on a sheep ranch in eastern Montana, which he escaped on the power of his beautiful tenor voice into a music scholarship and another life. After graduation he found his way to Northern, where he signed up for the occasional class as an excuse for hanging around the theater. He helped with makeup, he filled in as a director, he brought the audience to its feet when he sang the haunting Cossack solo in *Fiddler on the Roof*. But he had his own demons.

One night after a cast party at my house, the Peacock got in his car at dawn to drive home. He said afterward that he remembered driving up the hill to campus and making the turnaround Cowan Hall, then nothing until he woke up in broad daylight to see a fountain spraying his windshield. Apparently he had passed out and his car had jumped the curb and rolled across the lawn in front of Cowan Hall, narrowly missing some ornamental boulders but flattening several saplings before coming to a stop in the reflecting pool.

We all went to marvel at the deep trenches left by his tires across the freshly seeded lawn. It was a joke. The only ones who didn't think it was funny were the cops and the judge. The Peacock got a bawling out in court and a 150-dollar fine, and he went right on drinking as before.

The drinking. Five or six or seven Square Bottle Ditches a night in the Stockman's or the Red Lion or the Three Hundred Club. Driving home at three or four in the morning, crashing for a few hours. Shuddering awake to the alarm, waking Jack and Elizabeth for school, showering and driving back to campus to teach the composition classes I had taught so many times that I was beginning to teach them in my sleep. A meeting or two, another fight brewing over curriculum, plots and counterplots being laid against the technology faculty, alliances among the academic faculty being formed and dissolved in the endless political games played by daylight in Cowan Hall—*What kind of a college do they think this is? Why shouldn't a drafting student have to take an art class? Surely a diesel major needs some math?*—until I could escape downstairs to the familiar gurgling pipes and the odor of sweat and stale makeup in the windowless Little Theater, where any fantasy was possible.

The drinking! Wasn't that long-ago girl an adult, after all? Wasn't she setting her students a bad example in those soused hours after the long rehearsals, and was it any excuse that most of those students were in their twenties and thirties, close to her own age? (How would she have stopped their drinking, after all? If she had stayed home, they would simply have gone drinking without her.)

The drinking. There would come a night, three or four years in the future, when my second husband would come to the door of our bedroom, where I was asleep, to say, "You'd better get up and talk to this kid." And there would be Elizabeth, in her junior year of high school, white faced and vacant eyed, to tell of the beer party in the mountains and the four girls who had climbed in a jeep and roared back to town to confront somebody's boyfriend, and how they had missed a curve, and how Elizabeth and a friend had been the next on the scene, and how Elizabeth had held the hand of a girl who had been thrown from the jeep to hang on a barbed wire fence and die there. But that scene was yet to come, and in the meantime, in the shadows cast by the glittering back bar, I knew I was half in one world, half in another, both a part and apart, which was another reason why I was drawn to Trev, who didn't give a good goddamn what anybody else said or thought.

There was a story about Trev and one of his girlfriends; they had been engaged; he had given her a diamond ring. She decided to break off the engagement and tried to give him his ring back. The two of them were sitting in the cab of Trev's truck, somewhere out on the nightbound prairie. Trev took the ring and, to her horror, tossed it out the open window of the truck—I've got no use for it, he remarked.

I don't know what happened next. I like to imagine that the girl tumbled out of the truck and fell on her hands and knees, frantically groping in the dark through bunchgrass and cactus to recover the ring, while Trev waited for her to give up so he could give her a ride back to town. When she climbed back in the truck, ringless, her palms scored and bleeding, maybe he seemed heartless to her. He wasn't, though. There were reasons for his drunken nights and missed classes and long hours in the Little Theater, just as there were reasons for mine. He and I were both falling in love quite a lot in those days, although never with the right people, and never with each other.

Can that be true? It is true that I was never in love with Trev. We could be friends for some of the same reasons that the Peacock and I could be friends: because I felt no sexual pressure when I was with him, because I could hang out with him without anxiety, because Trev stood apart from that sick, repetitive dialogue between my husband and me.

Admit it! You're attracted to him.

No I'm not!

Admit it! You're having an affair with him.

I'm not!

Admit it! You're wishing *you were having an affair with him, which is just the same as.*

My husband had never taken Trev seriously, not sexually, and neither did I; and now I remember another fragment of overheard conversation, probably in the dressing room next to the Little Theater. "There's a man in here!" screamed one of the half-clad girls, then—"oh, never mind, it's only Trev."

"What does she think I am?" Trev asked later, half-laughing, but with a bitter edge. It is the bitter edge I hear now, in retrospect.

AND YET THAT MOMENT revolves with other moments, as though my memory were a kaleidoscope and every turn were random, every glimpse followed by another glimpse. Where is cause, where is effect, and when did the life of the Little Theater come to an end?

Flash and turn: the summer of 1973, when my husband comes back to Havre for sex with me and romance with the students. I've filed for divorce, but I've resisted having the final papers served; I suppose I still have hope in my old mantra, that we will be happy someday. I am walking at midnight with the Peacock along the hardpan shore of what passes for a lake. He and I have just gotten back from somewhere, perhaps from another town to see a film, and now we're in search of the drama crowd and the usual party. The air smells of the cattle that have left the deep imprints of their hoofs around the lake when they come down for water, and on the bluff behind us a bonfire is dying. The party must be over. Yes, here is everybody, sacked out in sleeping bags. And here is my husband, rolled up in a sleeping bag with one of the girls.

I'm shattered (although why should I have been?). The vast Highline sky is filled with stars, and the Peacock's arm is around me. *You'll be all right*, he's saying. *We've both been through worse.*

Flash and turn: I'm drunk out of my mind, which for me probably takes most of a fifth of Canadian Lord Calvert, and I'm in a pad at three in the morning, having left a cast party with one of the student actors. He's an asshole and I know he's an asshole, but I'm in his reeking bed with him, and he's rolled off and let me go, and I'm saying, *I love you, I love you, I love you*, and he's saying, *Yeah, well, I'm really tired.*

Then one night—Jack and Elizabeth mercifully away from home, staying at the ranch—my husband tracks me down at some guy's house, bursts through a door, punches me in the chin, and knocks me down. I sit on the floor, watching red and purple stars unfold, thinking they look just like an illustration from a Superman comic, while my husband rails: *Now I've got you just where I want you! On an adultery charge! You've got about five minutes to get yourself home! Serves you right if your jaw is broken! I should have hit you harder! Next time I'll hit you harder!*

The next morning I call the attorney, tell him to go ahead and have the papers served.

I'm out drinking with Trev when we run into a man named Bob Blew. He's a grown-up, several years older than I, and he has no connection at all with academe or theater, which seems to me a real plus. This particular night Bob sits down and drinks with us, and Trev offers him a ride home from the bar, so he's in the cab of Trev's truck with us when Trev pulls into my driveway to let me float up my back steps in the red dawn.

Did he kiss you good-night? asks a friend who knows I'm interested in Bob.

No, but Trev did, right in front of him.

What was Trev thinking, and was there a bitter edge?

In the spring of 1975, out of some momentary rage at the students or the college administrators—*serve them right if I weren't here to keep the theater going*—I had applied for a summer seminar in Houston, Texas, sponsored by the National Endowment for the Humanities to give professors at colleges like Northern a chance to work with a nationally recognized scholar. To my astonishment, Dr. Monroe K. Spears, Moody Professor of English at Rice University, selected my application. If I accepted, I would spend the summer studying the poetry of Robert Lowell with Dr. Spears in Houston, and the summer theater program at Northern would live or die under someone else's direction.

I was terrified at the thought of traveling to Houston to study with Dr. Spears. After five years teaching freshman composition and directing plays at Northern, I was no longer a scholar. I had lost all confidence in my research skills. True, I had written and published a handful of short stories, and I told myself I was writing regularly, but I wasn't. I was pouring all my energy into keeping the theater going, and for whose benefit? The life I had created under Cowan Hall was an illusion, and if I came blinking back upstairs into daylight, I was going to have to face what I had become.

I sent Jack and Elizabeth to the ranch for the summer, and Bob Blew flew me to Houston in his private airplane.

IN 2002 I DROVE eight hundred miles to Havre at the invitation of the Montana State Historical Society, which was holding its annual conference on Northern's campus. The town seemed shrunken to me, in the way the landscapes of one's youth always seem smaller than in memory. The Highline really has lost population; the farm crisis of the 1980s hit hard, and the grandchildren of those emigrant homesteaders, like Trev, have moved away to find a better way to earn a living. By contrast, the Northern campus and Cowan Hall looked spiffy with fresh paint and potted plants, although the college long ago lost its aspirations to a liberal arts curriculum and now focuses on teacher education and vocational-technical training.

The plenary events were scheduled in the Little Theater, where I had not set foot since leaving Montana almost two decades earlier. Like the rest of Cowan Hall, the theater had been completely renovated—new lighting, refurbished draperies, fine plush seating—although the college no longer offered a theater program of any kind. I wandered backstage, feeling the jolt of the past colliding with the daylight present. Where, for example, was the broken place in the off-stage drywall where, in *I Henry IV*, according to the original stage direction, "Douglas flieth," and the professor of history playing Douglas had flown, all right, into the inadequate wings and slam-bang into the intervening wall?

Patched and painted over, of course. Painted over were all the cast lists scribbled on the old drywall by students going back to the 1950s. Names well remembered, names half-forgotten, names of some I'm still in touch with. Falstaff directs high school musicals in Minnesota. Hotspur directs an academic program at a university in Iowa. Tillie (*The Effect of Gamma Rays on Man-in-the-Moon Marigolds*) teaches drama at a college in Colorado. Frank Butler (*Annie Get Your Gun*) teaches drama at a college in Virginia.

Mistress Quickly (*I Henry IV*) is dead of cancer. Ado Annie (*Oklahoma!*) is dead of emphysema. The poor Peacock, once the maid of honor at the Spokane drag queen ball, is dead these many years of AIDS.

Trev finally found the right girl and married her. They have three sons. Trev has had a movie career—watch for the dwarf in *Far and Away* and in *The Outlaw Josey Wales*—but his acting ambitions often collide with his other career as a gun dealer. After all, he is descended from Vikings. As for me, what can I say? For the past fifteen years I have been teaching at the University of Idaho in Moscow, mostly creative writing these days. I can't claim to have foregone fantasy in its entirety, but I have never again involved myself in play production.

Why? A long-ago night, a long-ago bar scene: I'm in tears, I've had too much to drink, and I've given way to self-pity for my failures in love and marriage, which I blame on being born with a brain and then insisting on educating that brain—"I'm a freak!" I sob.

Trev laughs his dry little cackle—"Don't feel like you're the only one," he says, and I'm stricken with shame, not just for what I've said, but for what I've let myself dissolve into.

THE LAST PLAY THAT Trev and I produced was *A Doll's House*. I played Nora's friend, Christine Linde, and Trev played Dr. Rank.

Ibsen may not have had a dwarf in mind when he conceived the character, but why not? Why not a young troll, deformed by his heredity and unlucky in love? I don't remember much about the production itself. Probably it creaked along with forgotten lines and clumsy staging, like most of our productions. I remember sitting and sewing on stage while a drunken Helmer leered at me, but I don't remember who played Helmer. What I do remember is Trev in act 3, when Dr. Rank recognizes that Nora will never love him and goes away to die. In that moment—and I can see Trev's white face as I write, I can see his shoulders hunched from his despair and from the ravaging of Dr. Rank's diseased spine. In that moment, I would like to believe something real happened, something approaching the artistry that in my heart of hearts I aspired to. In that moment I wish I had recognized the bitter edge.

8

Halfway between Havre and Great Falls, Montana, where Highway 87 crosses the Marias River, the tiny community of Loma nestles in the shade of shaggy cottonwood trees under a brow of steep bare bluffs. According to the 2000 census, a hundred people live here in a scatter of frame houses and a few mobile homes. In summer the sun sparkles on river current, dust blows down from the bluffs, and mirages retreat ever farther on the highway. In winter a powdery snow filters through the sagebrush, ice coats the highway, and the windchill factor drives the temperatures down to fifty below zero. There's still a post office somewhere in Loma, but nowhere to buy gas or groceries.

There is, however, the Loma Café. Low and rambling, the café turns a blank wall to the highway but opens to a small gravel parking lot off an unpaved street called Broadway. During the time I worked at Northern, those of us traveling back and forth to meetings or conferences in Great Falls or Missoula were drawn by that parking lot, if we had the time, to pull off the highway, turn off the ignition, and trudge through a litter of cottonwood twigs in summer or blown snow in winter to the storm doors that opened into lights and linoleum, a dozen tables, pastry in a glass counter, sizzle and scent of hot grease from the kitchen, and pots and pots of thin Western coffee. The Loma Café was a respite, a coffee break in another dimension, where for twenty or thirty minutes nobody had to think deep thoughts.

Two of Northern Montana College's nursing faculty had just pulled over at the Loma Café one day. Either they were on their way from Havre to Great Falls to observe their second-year students on clinical rotation at the Deaconess Hospital, or they were on their way back.

"See that trail up the bluff?" Sigrid pointed out to me during another, much later stop at the Loma Café, and I looked where she pointed at the single, nearly vertical track through the shale to the top of the bluff above the café. "Marjorie and I had just driven into the parking lot when some kid tried to make it all the way to the top on a motorcycle. He got about two-thirds of the way and pulled his motorcycle over backwards on himself. Marjorie and I leaped out of our car and ran."

I paused to picture Sigrid and Marjorie running up that nearly vertical track. Sigrid was in her sixties, a short squarely built woman with bouffant hair who favored matching coats and skirts and Hanes panty hose. Marjorie was younger and slimmer, but she also would have been wearing a dress with hose and heeled shoes. She and Sigrid didn't get along. They fought over curriculum and shot sparks off each other about everything from departmental procedures to nursing theory. But up there on the bluff was a motorcycle, upside down with its wheels spinning, and a kid who wasn't moving, and suddenly Sigrid and Marjorie were a professional team of nurses. See them run uphill in their good shoes! See them scramble as shale slides under them and they have to grab handfuls of bunchgrass to pull themselves along! Whoops, there's a misstep, a skinned knee, but no time to think about the ruined pair of panty hose. Is the kid breathing?

What with my fascination for the picture of Sigrid and Marjorie running uphill, I realize I've forgotten how badly hurt the boy was. I'm sure they told me, and my impression is that he needed some pretty extensive patching up. What I do know is how very lucky he was that it was Sigrid and Marjorie who pulled over at the Loma Café at the very moment he decided to try for the top of the bluff on his motorcycle.

ANY YOUNG PROFESSOR who came to Northern with an idea of higher education based on her own graduate experience had to think again. Ours was not the heady world of research grants, conference travel, or selective admission of students, but a world of our own creation where nobody outside our four-thousand-square-mile "service area" paid much attention to what we said or did. "Open admissions" meant that we accepted anyone who had graduated from a Montana high school, and we taught the students who came to us from the farms and ranches and small towns of the high prairie that stretches six hundred miles from Browning on the west edge of the Blackfeet Indian Reservation to Culbertson on the east edge of the Fort Peck Indian Reservation. For years many of these students planned to teach in Montana secondary schools and majored in English or history or biology. But in the early 1970s, word came that there was an oversupply of public schoolteachers and that new teachers weren't finding jobs. Students got the message, and, in a single year, enrollment at Northern dropped by nearly 20 percent.

Because state funding depended on enrollment, Northern was strapped. Faculty and staff were let go, the library budget was slashed, building and grounds maintenance delayed, and supplies rationed right down to the classroom chalk.

Enrollment gradually crept back up, but the mood and nature of the college had changed profoundly. We had lived through vicious blood-battles over which of us would keep our jobs and which would have to leave, and those who kept our jobs saw the empty offices and the faculty mailboxes from which names had been torn, and we remembered the innuendos and insults, and the floor fights over who should go and who should stay, and now we lived with unrelinquished grudges and vendettas and suspicions. Also we had been disabused of the fiction that we were teaching at Northern only for a few years until other, better jobs offered themselves. We knew now, although we kept it secret from each other, that better jobs weren't going to be offered to people who had been isolated and out of touch with their fields of study for years. For us there would be no other jobs. We were lucky to have kept the jobs we had, and so we hung on by teeth and claws, and we watched our backs.

Our students, too, seemed to have changed. From time out of memory, professors have complained about a decline in their students' preparation and interest, but after the erosion of teacher education programs at Northern, we were attracting students who cared little about "education" in the sense that most of us understood the word, but rather were looking for training in skills that would help them find jobs. They sat sullenly in the precollege composition classes that were supposed to improve their punctuation and grammar and wondered why they had to take English. Some of their major instructors seemed to agree with them, fueling suspicions that curriculum was being structured to provide job security for technology professors and leaving liberal arts professors out in the cold.

What else did we have to complain about? Well, we were slogging through the midseventies of the Carter administration. The war in Vietnam was over, but there was an oil embargo and an energy crisis and all our thermostats were turned down. There was a national recession of the economy, and there was inflation, and yet our salaries stayed the same. No money, no money anywhere in the university system. Interest rates soared so high that a friend, noting the temperature on a bank's marquee one hot day, remarked that it must be reflecting the prime rate.

I felt increasingly discouraged and isolated during those years. Divorced, juggling bills to make ends meet, trying to keep the peace among the English department faculty, I was teaching the same classes over and over to what seemed like the same students turning in the same disorganized essays. I knew I was drifting farther and farther away from my discipline. I heard rumors of exciting new literary theories being translated from the French, but even when I could get my hands on a book or two, I was mystified by what I read. What in the world, for example, was *aporia*? Or *différance*? All I could be certain of was that the New Critics I had read as an undergraduate were hopelessly old-fashioned and wrong, and so, by extension, was I. I look back at myself now and think: unwilling students, a failed marriage, an eroded paycheck, an inability to understand Jacques Derrida, who wouldn't feel discouraged?

So how did I, in my boredom and discouragement, with my PhD in English literature, with my dissertation that traced the influences of Latin satire on the comedies of Ben Jonson, become a dean of nursing?

Into our stew of discontent had come a new college president, all smiles. Dr. Erickson. He ensconced himself in the big office on the first floor of Cowan Hall, where white prairie light flooded the windows and dappled the desk and bookcases and rugs with the moving shadows of cottonwood leaves, and announced an open-door policy. After a few weeks of listening to an endless litany of grievances ranging from the time of day somebody was expected to teach his classes, the hostility of somebody's department chairman who had assigned his favorite class to another professor, the utter inadequacy of a colleague's syllabus, the lack of students in classes they ought to be taking, the failure of the college to finance a crucial field trip, and the never-to-be-forgotten sins of past college administrators, President Erickson's smile became fixed. Perhaps as a buffer for himself, perhaps to distract his quarreling faculty, he decided to reorganize the college into schools, each with a dean.

I was to turn over the chairmanship of the English department to someone else and become the Dean of Arts and Sciences. Because the new president wished the schools to be approximately equal in size, he moved the nursing department out of its traditional home in technology and assigned it to me. The nurses were just as surprised as I was by the move, and I think even more apprehensive.

A SCENE FROM MEMORY: the nursing faculty has gathered in my office for our first meeting. It must be early fall in Havre, because leaves still dapple the light falling from the big west windows. We are sitting around my long oak conference table (another embarrassing perk of being a dean: when I complained about the scars on the table, the physical plant sent somebody right over to refinish it), myself and Sigrid and Marjorie and Joan and Emily, the nursing department chairperson. Emily is about fifteen years older than I am. She was the only female chairperson on campus until I became a chairperson. That's what she and I are called, chairpersons. The male chairmen are called chairmen. Now I'm the dean, and everyone is nervous.

If these women seem staid and conservative to me in their coats and skirts and their world of practical applications, I must seem outlandish, even alarming. For one thing, the nurses have always been housed over in the technology building, and they identify with the technology faculty, for whom we in the liberal arts are dangerous elitists with scholarship in subjects nobody in their right minds would waste time on (influences of Latin satire on Ben Jonson's comedies, for example). Also, although I had settled down from the days right after my divorce, when I had hung out with the theater students and closed the local bars most nights, I probably still carried the reputation of the campus wild child. Miniskirt, makeup, that was me.

I don't remember what the nurses and I discussed that first day, although I assume they filled me in on the crisis in nursing education that would occupy our next several years. What I do remember is that I had placed a pot of ivy in the center of the oak conference table, and the ivy wasn't doing well. Marjorie, the nurse nearest to me in age, began picking dead leaves off the ivy. By the end of the meeting, a little mound of dead leaves had risen on the table in front of her, and none of us could focus on anything but her leaf picking.

A few years later, when I knew Marjorie better, the other nurses and I stopped at her house to pick her up for one of our regular visits down to the second-year clinical students at the Deaconess Hospital in Great Falls. Marjorie lived a few miles south of town in a pleasant house shaded by cottonwoods and surrounded by pastureland. As I waited in the car for her, I noticed a large tree stump in her front yard, apparently attached to an IV stand with a drip bag and tubing.

"Marjorie," I said as she climbed into the car, "do you think you can save that stump? It looks terminal to me."

She looked embarrassed. "I was out of town for several days," she explained, "and I knew my husband wouldn't water my houseplants. So I brought them out here on the stump and fixed them up with a drip. I can set the drip to however much water the plants need, and it works a treat."

PEOPLE USED TO ASK me why I wanted to be a dean. Sometimes I said I did it for the money, which was partly true. As a dean, I was paid a starting salary of $27,000 (it was 1977, after all, and I had been making less than $20,000 as a professor). Now, with a typically bloated administrative salary, as one of the professors in my old department called it, I could pay my bills on time.

Another reason, also partly true, but which I usually left unstated, was the pressure the women's groups at that time were putting on academic women to move up the administrative ladder. These were the heady days when there were still hopes for the ratification of the Equal Rights Amendment (or fears of its ratification, in the case of a lot of people in Montana), and I got letters and phone calls pointing out how rare were the opportunities for women to become administrators in higher education and how fortunate I was to be in a position to take that first step. The plan would be to hold the dean's post for four or five years and then apply for deanships at larger colleges or perhaps academic vice presidencies at small ones; the main thing would be to keep moving, and, with great good luck, end up in a large dappled office listening to faculty complaints with a fixed smile that only the thought of retirement would allow to relax.

The pressure groups for affirmative action did succeed in getting more women interviewed, if not hired, for positions in higher education. In the early 1980s, after our smiling president announced his retirement, we brought a woman to campus to consider for his position. She had been carefully coached by the kinds of women who had phoned or written to me; I recognized the carefully planned phraseology. She had had a fresh manicure for the occasion of the interview, but she clearly was nervous. I watched her short magenta fingernails as she clutched her hands and recited her talking points—"My goal is to become president of a college—and I *will* become president of a college, I've determined that goal—the only question is *where*—"

"They'd eat her alive here," said one of the men when she left the room. I have often wondered what became of her.

What motives were left besides money and ambition? Boredom with repetitive teaching, certainly. Also there was the illusion of power, fostered by the small perks of administrative life; for example, the physical plant would send a carpenter right over to replace a dean's cabinet hinge, when faculty had been pleading for laboratory repairs for months. Most seductive of all, though, like an ever-receding mirage of water on a summer highway, was altruism: the possibility making a real contribution to the college.

Altruism, say the geneticists, always can be traced back to self-preservation, or the so-called selfish gene. I can't argue with their premise, but I do believe that altruism was what kept Northern Montana College operating from its shaky beginnings in the 1930s through the depression and the recession and the years when a state blue-ribbon commission voted to shut the campus down, and the years when it appeared as though the state legislature was set on starving the place to death by cutting its funding. Older professors remembered lending money to students to keep them in school. They remembered building lockers for the athletic squads out of lath and chicken wire. Everyone complained, but somehow an extra student always got squeezed into a lab class, somehow the necessary coursework got on the schedule, somehow programs were held together. Departments fought with each other over curriculum with the ferocity of Balkan states defending their borders, but let an outsider call for closure and everyone was ready to sign the petitions or travel down to the state capitol to protest. Truth was, most of us had invested so much of ourselves in Northern Montana College that we felt as though we owned it. Shabby, starving, and looked down upon, we were Northern Montana College, and Northern Montana College was ours, and by god, we were going to keep the place running.

So there I was, listening to professors complain so the president didn't have to listen to them. I felt desperate for meaningful work, and what I got was the nursing department.

AT THE TIME OF our first meeting, the day Marjorie picked all the dead leaves off the ivy plant, the nursing faculty had just received a couple of very serious blows. First and most immanent, they had been warned by the Montana Board of Nursing that they were in danger of losing their accreditation if they did not immediately correct a number of deficiencies. Second, and equally dire to the future of their program, they had learned that the National League for Nursing was recommending a baccalaureate degree as the minimum qualification for all registered nurses.

Some background: for many years, young women and the occasional young man who wished to become registered nurses, or RNs, could choose one of three kinds of programs. A popular option, especially for poor or working-class women, was to sign up for a diploma program at a local hospital where they would receive on-the-job training for two or three years and then receive their caps and pins. Diploma programs stressed the practical applications of nursing procedures, and, by all accounts, supplied excellent nurses for many years. But by the late 1970s, when I got involved in nursing education, most of the diploma programs nationwide were being phased out.

Another option was to enroll at a community college, or at a four-year institution like Northern Montana College, where students took general education classes on campus and went on to get hospital, or clinical experience, leading to an associate degree in nursing, which qualified them to sit for the state nursing boards. These programs were intense, they provided solid hands-on training, and they allowed new nurses to get out of school, get to work and start paying back their student loans after two years and a summer (or three years, if the student nurses wanted time to catch their breaths between classroom and clinic). These were the associate degree programs, like Northern's, that would be phased out of existence if the National League for Nursing followed through on its recommendation that a baccalaureate degree would become the sole path to the RN.

Emily wrung her hands. "It's so unrealistic! How will small hospitals ever be able to afford baccalaureate nurses? Where will they find enough baccalaureate nurses?"

There were two baccalaureate programs in nursing in Montana at that time, one at Carroll College, a private Catholic college in Helena, and the other at Montana State University in Bozeman. Emily, of course, knew the directors of both nursing programs and was awed by them. Both sat on the Montana Board of Nursing, which was threatening to revoke our accreditation, and it didn't take people as paranoid as we at Northern to suspect that political maneuvering was going on.

I mean, Montana State University! Big time! They knew and we knew they were big time, and one of the reasons they were big time was because we were so little and no-account, and that was how they were going to keep us. Not just in nursing, but all over Northern, professors griped about classes they taught that the faculty over at MSU wouldn't accept for transfer credit. In the case of nursing coursework, the reasons why our associate degree graduates couldn't transfer into the MSU baccalaureate program had to do with some of the reasons the state board was threatening our accreditation.

"Sigrid teaches the exact same class in nutrition that they teach over there," Emily explained to me. "She uses the same textbook they use. But they won't accept her class for transfer credit because she doesn't have a BSN, that is, a baccalaureate degree in nursing. She has a diploma in nursing, and she has BS and MS degrees in counseling and guidance."

Requirement number 1 for accreditation: faculty with appropriate degrees in the areas of their professions. Sigrid had her degrees in counseling and guidance for reasons having to do with location and circumstance. Her husband was a Lutheran minister, now retired and in ill health, and Sigrid simply hadn't had the wherewithal to go off to Bozeman for the time it would have taken her to earn BSN and MSN degrees. She was a thorough, even formidable, teacher in the classroom and in clinical, but alas, she was uncertified for what she was teaching.

Requirement number 2 for accreditation: to adopt and articulate a coherent nursing theory, with "threads" running down from the goals of our theory down through teaching objectives and tied to specific classroom or clinical experience. I didn't know a thing about "threads," let alone nursing theory, but I read the narrative Emily had submitted to the state board of nursing, noted its inconsistencies, and realized that the problem here wasn't *aporia*, but language that needed to be grounded and specific and that meant what it said. The one thing I could do for Emily and Sigrid and Joan and Marjorie was to lend them my writing skills.

FORTUNATELY EMILY, as the director of the program, had BSN and MSN degrees. The faculty at the Deaconess Hospital in Great Falls thankfully had their degrees, and one of them was beginning a doctoral program in nursing, which would be a great advantage to us. Sigrid and Joan would be retiring in a year or two, and in the meantime we scoured the country for qualified faculty and found Sister, a habitless nun with a hair-trigger temper but the requisite degrees in nursing, and Louise, a sweet Seventh-Day Adventist who drew the line only at supervising clinical shifts on Saturdays. Department meetings became quite ecumenical.

By this time I was becoming an extremely partisan dean of nursing. In all my experience in higher education, undergraduate and graduate and postgraduate, I had never met women like these nurses. For years before I startled the campus by showing up in my miniskirt and false eyelashes, before I annoyed people by arguing for the ratification of the Equal Rights Amendment and insisting on a teaching schedule that was just as reasonable as the schedules the men got, these women had quietly gone about their work of preparing their students to pass rigorous state nursing board examinations and enter a demanding profession. At a time when some on campus seriously questioned whether women really could teach English at the college level, no one questioned whether women could teach nursing. Of course they could!

None of the nurses had had easy lives. Marjorie told how, as a young woman, she was allowed by her husband (the same husband who, years later, wouldn't water her houseplants while she was away from home) to work as a hospital nurse as long as she took care of their four children and kept a perfect house. "I would work my shift," she said, "pick up the kids, feed them, and get them to bed. Then I'd stay up all night doing housework. Along about four in the morning, I'd pop speed and take a bath and sleep for an hour before I had to get up and be on shift at the hospital at six."

Emily's husband had been in medical school when Pearl Harbor was bombed. He ended up in France, where he was blinded by shrapnel. For a few years after he healed, he tended a candy counter at the local post office, but it didn't bring in enough to make ends meet, so Emily went back to college, got her degrees, and began teaching at Northern. She had been the mainstay of the family ever since.

Sigrid and her husband had trained as missionaries and were set to sail for China in 1937 when the Japanese invaded. If they had sailed a few weeks earlier, they probably would have been captured and interned for the duration. As it was, they stayed in America, but in the meantime Sigrid had learned to speak and read Chinese in spite of having been told it would be too difficult. Her method, she said, was to write a single Chinese character on a note card, then carry a stack of the note cards around with her. Whenever she had a free moment, waiting for a bus perhaps, or for a pot to boil, she would take out a card and memorize another character. When she pulled out her cards in the middle of one of her husband's sermons—"You've gone too far this time," she recalled him telling her.

AFTER WHAT SEEMED LIKE endless meetings, everyone agreed that they wanted to base their program on the nursing theory developed by Martha Rogers in the 1960s. I began reading about Rogers's model, which "focuses on the individual as a unified whole in constant interaction with the environment," and shook my head, but Emily and Sigrid were patient with me. They pointed out that the general concept of a nursing model wasn't as complicated as it sounded. If your model focused on illness, for example, your curriculum would differ from a curriculum based on a model that focused on wellness. A model that focused solely on the patient obviously would differ from a model like Rogers's, which takes into account the patient's family, community, environment, and spirituality.

I told myself that at least Martha Rogers wasn't as impenetrable as Jacques Derrida, and I set to work. It has been over twenty-five years now, and I have had little occasion to contemplate nursing theory during those years, and as I have rethought my experience as a dean of nurses, I realize how much I have forgotten about Martha Rogers and her nursing theory, let alone the nursing theories of Imogene King or Dorothea Orem or the many others we considered. I will say for myself that, at the time I finished our narrative for the state board of nursing, I knew more about nursing theory than any nonnursing professional that Emily and Sigrid and Joan and Marjorie, at least, had ever known. Indeed, I think they came to be proud of me. They speculated that, if they could just figure out a way to sneak me into the state nursing board exams (which they couldn't, because I would have to have graduated from an accredited nursing program), I would pass the written part of the exams. I felt a mild regret at never having the chance to find out.

ONCE WE HAD "addressed our deficiencies" and no longer faced the dire prospect of losing our accreditation from the state board of nursing, we had to consider what would become of us if the National League for Nursing really did pull the plug on associate degree nursing programs. The answer seemed pretty obvious to me.

"We need to start a baccalaureate program."

Emily anguished over the prospect. "I just don't think we *ought* to! I don't think they'd *let* us! The baccalaureate programs have *always* been in Bozeman and Helena. They don't *want* us to have a baccalaureate program."

I felt impatient with Emily. I had come to admire her quiet professionalism; she was gracious with colleagues, warm with students, thoughtful and informed and hard working. So why did she feel so humble? Whose permission did she think she needed? But I plowed on, and with varying degrees of apprehension the nurses followed. First on our agenda: to wring money out of the college president to hire us a consultant from the National League for Nursing. The president agreed; he was as anxious as anyone not to lose the nursing program. So out to Havre, Montana, came a lovely woman from darkest New York City. She got her bearings after what she described as a harrowing two-mile drive from the local airport through open prairie, looked over our curriculum, and listened to our woes.

"What you need," she said at last, "is a multi-entry, multi-exit nursing program. Such a program allows nurses to leave at the associate degree level—or even at the licensed practical nursing level—work in the field for a while, then return and, without having to repeat classes or clinical experiences, move directly into the baccalaureate program. With such a program, you can draw working nurses who wish to take that next step in their profession. Unfortunately, a multi-entry, multi-exit program is also the most difficult to design."

We looked at each other. We'd come this far.

THE DIFFICULTY IN DESIGNING a multi-entry, multi-exit nursing program is that the various forms of nursing education—licensed practical nursing, diploma nursing, associate degree nursing, baccalaureate degree nursing—are designed to turn out graduates who will do distinctly different work, ranging from the most basic to the more theoretical and decision-making levels. A multi-entry, multi-exit nursing program isn't exactly analogous to, say, a program for transforming journeymen carpenters into architects, but that's the general idea. Because baccalaureate programs are likely to expect their graduates to become supervisors or administrators in larger hospitals, they tend not to stress the direct hands-on clinical experience found in an associate degree program. Emily told, with a certain pride, how she had had to coach her own daughter, a graduate of the Montana State baccalaureate program, in giving injections.

Redesigning a nursing program for multi-entry, multi-exit means that the faculty must be willing to rethink their ideas of how nursing education is supposed to progress. They have to compromise, they have to be willing to take risks, they have to find ways around preconditions they had thought were immutable. On the other hand, such a program can be a great gift to the working nurse at the diploma or associate degree level who wants to earn a BSN without starting at the beginning. (It's also a great gift to the college administrator who suddenly sees a whole new pool of potential students.)

And so we worked for two years to "describe our model" and "draw our threads" to connect our goals and objectives to our curriculum. My job was to keep everyone on task and write up the results. Emily and Sigrid and the other nurses were always patient with me, explaining at length about some arcane detail or other about their profession; they were teachers, after all. But I wasn't a nursing student, I would never be a nurse, and if we succeeded in our quest, the baccalaureate program would be theirs, not mine. In a murky way I knew but never admitted that I was becoming a kind of shadow. The closest I've come since to a similar feeling has been as the silent editor of someone else's book. Perhaps a professional ghostwriter would understand that sense of self and shadow.

It wasn't just the nursing. Being a dean was turning me into a person I didn't really like. Academic administration has its own arcane language of hints and codes and what is known in the diplomatic world as double tracking; that is, saying one thing and doing another. When I came across a character in a C. P. Snow novel who remarked that a certain politician had achieved his lofty position by teaching himself never to utter an unconsidered word, I realized something about the life I had wandered into. Language—words—mattered to me. I had come to Northern Montana College with an idea of myself as a scholar. But—out of touch, three hundred miles from a university library, and of course without the Internet resources that exist today—I had turned to writing fiction. I published a handful of short stories and then a collection of stories, and I thought of writing a novel. Now that I was a dean, I kept a typewriter behind my desk, and I rattled on it at odd moments. Oh yes, I'm writing, I told people, and I was—I wrote grants, I wrote catalog copy, I wrote memos, I wrote proposals, and God knows I wrote a multi-entry, multi-exit nursing program, but in the ten years I was a dean I did not write a word of fiction worth keeping.

EMILY CONTINUED TO FEEL uneasy about our plans, which seemed to violate some deep sense of hers about the great chain of being in nursing education in Montana, and she probably felt grateful that she would be on sabbatical leave while Sigrid and I presented our proposal to the state board of nursing and asked for their blessing. I might have shared some of Emily's unease if I had not been so absorbed in the proposal that I hardly felt the direction of the blowing wind and never saw that our known world of Northern was beginning to crumble and be replaced by something new.

President Erickson had finally retired and was replaced by a man whose ideas for the campus were far less altruistic than President Erickson's had been. "I've never been a president before, and I want to be a *good* president," President Erickson used to say, and he had done what he could. He probably understood that the carping and tattling and petty complaints from his professors were symptoms of the larger disorder, and he had listened, he had soothed, he found the loose change to purchase small necessities like classroom chalk, and he stumped across our four thousand square miles of "service area" explaining to elderly immigrant farmers the tax advantages of leaving some of their property to Northern Montana College in their wills. He spoke a little Norwegian, and sometimes he charmed these old men and women by speaking to them in the language of their childhoods, and in small part he made up for the stinginess of state funding through their donations.

Then, just about the time the new president arrived, another financial disaster hit Montana, this time in the form of the farm crisis of the 1980s. As the state's tax base dried up, legislators guarded the general fund as though they expected it to blow away with the drought wind. The old refrain—*no money, no money, anywhere*—had reached a hysterical pitch when Sigrid and I drove down to Helena to make our presentation to the state board of nursing.

I try to remember the details of that cramped conference room in the Department of Education building, and I come up with fragments far less precise than the dead leaves Marjorie picked off my ivy plant on that fall day so long ago. By that time I knew most of the women who sat on the state board of nursing, had had verbal skirmishes with some of them, knew that some of them were legendary for their brave work on behalf of nursing in Montana, and yet not a face, not a name returns to me. The details of the room also have faded, but it does seem to me that the light was too dim even to cast shadows. Had a storm blown over the mountains that afternoon, had the window darkened with an overcast sky?

Sigrid sat at the head of the conference table and spoke, while I sat on a folding chair to one side and observed. I don't remember a word she said, but I can see Sigrid clearly: squarely built and corseted, her hair dyed an aggressive auburn, she showed no outward signs of nervousness as she outlined our plans. In contrast with the presidential candidate who had clutched her magenta-tipped fingers, Sigrid's hands were clean and clipped and steady. Hands that cooked the most renowned Chinese food in northern Montana, hands that had busied themselves on our drive down to Helena correcting the student bib cards she carried in her purse, just as she had once carried cards of Chinese characters to memorize. Just the hands you'd want tending you if you happened to pull your motorcycle over backwards on yourself.

"You did wonderfully," I told her, once we were alone in the corridor.

The Lutheran pastor's wife gave me a grim look. "That's the power of prayer," she said.

She and I drove back to Havre in muted elation. We had felt some hostility in the boardroom, but we also knew we were had accomplished what we set out to do. Indeed, the formidable director of nursing at Montana State University had told me, "We think it's going to be difficult for you, but we wish you luck."

We got home to find the campus in an uproar that drowned out any excitement about the prospects of a baccalaureate degree in nursing. Deeper funding cuts! Northern Montana College was unlikely to survive! Could it be saved? If so, how? The new president's strategy was a sweeping, across-the-board elimination of administrative and staff positions that would demonstrate to the state legislature how dire were the straits and how determined he was to keep the campus from going under. Gone would be the director of the physical plant, gone would be the director of the learning center and his staff, gone would be the librarian, gone would be the registrar, and gone would be the deans. I would have a choice between going back to teaching precomposition courses in the English department and finding another job. Nobody wanted to hear about Sigrid's and my success with the board of nursing. Success at this juncture was almost a badge of shame.

AFTER EMILY RETURNED from sabbatical, she and I sat and drank coffee one last time in the Loma Café. Maybe we were on our way home from some errand at the Deaconess Hospital in Great Falls. Maybe it was late spring and the sun sparkled on the river, and the motorcycle tracks cut deep furrows into the vertical bluff, and maybe we were getting ready to graduate another class of associate degree nurses.

"I was daydreaming," I told Emily. "In my daydream, we got the baccalaureate program approved, and everyone was very happy about it."

"That was a nice daydream," said Emily.

I think now about the traumas of Emily's life, how she got the news that her young husband had been wounded on a European battlefield, how the surgeons gave her hope that they could save the sight in one of his eyes, how that hope turned out to be cruel. How she picked up the pieces of their lives and carried on. Don't ask for more than you have—was that the lesson she learned? Or had she learned, long before I did, how much success can cost?

I HAVEN'T KEPT TRACK of the twists or turns that nursing education has taken during the more than twenty years since Sigrid presented our baccalaureate program to the state board, although I do know that the National League for Nursing never did follow through with their plans to eliminate associate degree RN programs. As Emily had foreseen, the baccalaureate programs alone would never fill the need for registered nurses. To this day, the majority of working nurses have been trained at the associate degree level. However, multi-entry, multi-exit programs that provide student nurses with the options of going to work after two years and eventually returning for another two years seem to have blossomed in colleges and universities throughout the nation. A quick browse through Web sites finds many such programs urging me to look into the opportunities they can provide, even promising that I can complete a baccalaureate nursing degree on line.

Northern still has its multi-entry, multi-exit baccalaureate nursing program, although the college has lost its separate identity and now is a satellite campus of Montana State University. I wonder about the relationship between the respective departments of nursing. Are the nurses of MSU-Northern looked down upon and expected to be appropriately humble? I don't recognize any of their names, except for the current director, who is an old friend. She completed her associate degree in nursing under the direction of Emily and Sigrid and Marjorie and Joan. She married, had a daughter, and was divorced. She worked as a hospital nurse for several years and then returned to campus to complete her baccalaureate degree. Eventually, with a master's degree in nursing, she joined the Northern faculty, and now she's at the helm.

Having my dean's chair kicked out from under me was the best thing that could have happened to me, although it didn't feel like it at the time. Once I was teaching again, that life of grants and contracts and nursing proposals and the arcane, guarded language of academic administration gradually faded like the shadow it was, and I found my way back to writing fiction.

9

THE MALE ANIMAL, lonely and embittered, tests the bars of his confinement. Bellows his anger. Nobody loves him. When he was very young his head was fondled, soft words spoken, a bucket held for him to drink. Now he weighs nearly two tons, and everyone is afraid of him, and yet he is helpless and penned. His dark muscles ripple as he bows his neck and paws the dirt. He might root at the ground he stands on, if it were not for the pain of the ring they have fixed in his nose to control him. Between his legs hang the secret sac of jewels and the sheathed rod that are the reasons for his existence. Again he bellows, turning his head for something to gore. He is the most dangerous animal in the world. Soon they will be coming to kill him.

THE MAN WE CAME to call Studly behind his back was in his forties, with a head of springy dark hair and a dark moustache that obscured a slight defect in his upper lip. He was tall and fit and bronzed from lots of sun or—it would be whispered—from a lot of time under a sunlamp. He had the well-developed chest of a rugby player—it was said that he had played football in college—and he always seemed on the verge of bursting from musculature or exuberance out of his blue business suit and white shirt and tie.

When he made his first speech to the assembled faculty and students, I came late for some reason, and I sat, not in the semicircle of folding chairs around the podium, but on a low brick ledge that framed one side of the ballroom. I wasn't paying attention to what he was saying. Content is beside the point and potentially dangerous in these kinds of presentations; the trick is to compliment your audience, project your personality, and avoid the kinds of sound bytes that will ring in the ears of the presidential search committee when they sit down to assess the candidates. Studly, with his physical presence and his self-deprecating humor, was an adept. I watched the faces soften, the mouths grow slack, sophomores and senior professors and student life staff falling under the spell of Studly's charm. Gradually I became aware that he had spotted me on my brick ledge. He was throwing me glances, playing to me in body language. If we'd been in a bar instead of the student union ballroom, if I hadn't believed it of a man who was interviewing to be the next president of Northern, I would have thought he was hitting on me.

I've studied a snapshot of myself, taken on campus at about that time, trying to get a glimpse of the woman Studly saw in the spring of 1984. She looks very young to me now, younger than she really was, which was about Studly's own age. Slim and trim in the blue polyester pantsuit that was standard wear for a woman in academic administration in those days, dark haired and, well, pretty. Pretty is not how she felt. A clue to how she felt is in the snapshot, in the way her arms are folded, her face averted. Aloof, someone might have described her.

BY 1984 IT SOMETIMES seemed as though all of us at Northern were at each other's throats. Colleagues blamed colleagues for gerrymandered curricula and the theft of students from one department into another, and they blamed the college administration for the penny-pinching that had eliminated all travel or enrichment funds and pared budgets for supplies to the bone. No one had had a raise in pay in years.

For their part, the college's beleaguered administrators seemed to think the faculty were a whining lot who taught only twelve or fifteen hours a week and refused to accept more than thirty students in a freshman composition class or more than twenty students in a chemistry lab that contained only twenty lab stations. Listening to administrators discuss the faculty, or listening to the faculty discuss the administration was like listening to two sides of an acrimonious divorce. There was no explaining to my fellow administrators how much time it took to read and grade 150 freshman essays. All I got were tolerant smiles. Nor was there any explaining to my former colleagues on the faculty that there were no secret hoards of cash on campus. They thought I was complicit with the rest of the scoundrels.

President Erickson was looking forward to his retirement. The rest of us looked forward to his replacement, whoever that might be. A change, any change, would at least be a distraction and—who could tell?—might put us back on the road to solvency and academic respectability and full rosters of liberal arts majors.

We could dream, couldn't we?

While President Erickson listened to endless complaints, the dean of students took charge of the campus. She spent a lot of time with the faculty union's collective bargaining team, haggling over pay raises (highly unlikely) and procedures for layoffs (only too likely). These sessions seemed to go on for weeks, while time stood still and nothing else could be accomplished. "She and the bargaining team need each other," remarked one of the academic vice presidents who came to the campus for a year or two and left.

The fact was, there was no money anywhere. The years of Jimmy Carter's presidency had brought gas shortages and recession, and our isolated northern prairie region had been stricken by drought and farm foreclosures. Tax revenues were lower than projected, and the state's general fund was depleted. No money, not for the university system and certainly not for our tiny campus. As budgets were whittled back and programs curtailed, we began to wonder which was more likely, a sudden closure of the college we loved or its slow death by starvation.

Love. Not too strong a word for the way most of us—faculty, staff, administrators, students—felt about the college. Like many others, I felt as though I owned the place. I had worked so hard, designing and teaching courses, founding a theater program, taking on the deanship against my better judgment, cheering all our small achievements and discounting our setbacks, and telling myself that surely the future wouldn't be so bad, surely there would be ways to attract students, surely some pendulum would swing back to support the liberal arts.

"Institutions thrive on the work of people like you," a friend warned me. "An institution will take all you have to give, and when you've given and given until you have nothing left, the institution will cast you aside, because after all, it's an institution, and institutions don't care."

But now, as the Carter years came to an end and Ronald Reagan arrived at the White House with his theory of trickle-down economics, surely change was now at hand.

So, Studly.

"Was he attractive?" asked a friend, recently, when I told her the story.

I hesitated. "He was handsome," I finally said. "Handsome and vibrant. And lots of people—lots of women—found him attractive."

But I never was attracted to him. The reason had nothing to do with my judgment, everything to do with *never again*.

~

Studly and his wife moved into the presidential mansion, which looked into the teeth of the wind from a hill above the town and campus. The wife was a very pretty young blonde woman who favored tailored suits that looked a bit too old for her, and she had brought along her bamboo and rattan furniture from a southern climate. I never knew her well. On the one or two occasions that I attended receptions at the mansion, I thought how she and her tropical upholstery contrasted with the shortgrass prairie landscape beyond her windows. She wasn't Studly's first wife.

Studly's office on campus seemed little changed from the days when the old president kept his door open. You walked up a short flight of stone steps that led to the first floor of Cowan Hall, through the heavy double front doors, and down a ringing granite corridor past the registrar's office and the business office to a glass wall that protected the president and the vice president and the dean of students from the rest of the world. I clattered down from the second floor one day on my high-heeled dean's shoes, on some errand, perhaps with the vice president's secretary, and encountered Studly strolling out of his office with his muscles rippling under his blue suit and his hands clasped behind his back.

He ran his eyes over me.

"You're looking very good," he murmured. "That outfit is very well chosen."

"Thanks," I said, looking around for escape. I was wearing a gray gabardine suit with a bluish sweater I'd thrown on that morning in between getting two-year-old Rachel ready for day care, answering phone calls, trying to placate people my husband owed money to, and losing and finally finding the agenda for my meeting with my department chairs.

"Blue is good," Studly said. "So is gray."

"Really?"

"Oh, yes. Blue and gray are power colors. They're your best choices to project your image."

I was nonplussed by the caressing voice, the eyes that roved over me. Instinctively I moved back. "I never think about image," I said, which was true. Also, to receive wardrobe advice from a college president was beyond my experience.

"Oh, you should! Image is very important!"

He had moved so close to me that I could smell the male odors of soap and cologne and something darker and damper than tobacco, an odor I couldn't place. The whites of his eyes were clear in his bronzed face, his chest very broad under the expanse of white shirt and jutting necktie, his fingernails very clean. I looked away, I saw the glass doors leading to the corridor, and I said something, perhaps as inane as, "I'll think about my image," and turned and fled, leaving him standing there.

"Be careful," our current vice president warned me. "He doesn't like you."

"Why?"

"I don't know. He doesn't say it outright." The vice president paused and thought for a moment. "Because you're aloof."

My office had become my sanctuary. It was a large room on the second floor of Cowan Hall, with tall west-facing windows and a polished oak library table where I could sit in meetings with the department chairmen, and it was lined with the books I had been carting around for years. I had a desk and a swivel chair and a side table where I kept a typewriter and, in odd moments, tried and failed to write fiction. A door behind my desk opened into the foreign language laboratory, and another door opened into an outer office, where my secretary, who had once been my student, presided over an appointment book and a computer and visited with the faculty who came in to help themselves to coffee. I kept a can of Pledge and a dustcloth in a drawer, and sometimes I dusted my books and the oak table and the windowsills and watered the plants and kept the room in order. It was, I sometimes thought, the only order in my life.

Bob had come back from Kansas, fragile and demented from his untreated pulmonary fibrosis, with a single purpose: keeping me from divorcing him. He was sure I must have a lover. Why else would I file for divorce? If I didn't drop the suit, he would take Rachel, and I would never see her again.

"You have to take his threat seriously," said my attorney. "You have to get a restraining order."

I was terrified that every shadow might materialize into him, that he might pounce on Rachel and disappear with her, as he had vowed. I didn't think what worse he might have done until, years later, the attorney who had represented me in my divorce suit told me that Bob had called him at work and threatened to shoot out his windows—"I had small children," said the attorney, "so I called the police and tore home. The police picked him up a block from my house, with guns in his car."

"You never told me."

"No. I thought you had enough to worry about."

Forbidden by law from having any contact with me, Bob haunted the campus. He disguised himself with a woman's scarf tied over his head and drove a borrowed car around and around the administration hall, hoping to catch me with my lover. Seeing nothing but the curious glances of students, he parked the car and tottered, gasping, up the stairs to the second floor, where my secretary spotted him and locked the door between her office and mine. Cowering behind my desk, I listened to his feverish questions.

"Where is she? What do you mean, you don't know?"

SOMEHOW, SOMEHOW, work got done. I was reviewing sheets of enrollment figures one afternoon when Studly burst into my office.

"Some might think it funny, but you'd better know that I don't think it's funny at all!"

He was red with rage, forcing his words through gritted teeth. I couldn't think what he was talking about.

"That toilet is not funny, and I'll get the one who put it there!"

It finally dawned on me. The green toilet.

The green toilet happened because our university system was so pared and exhausted of funding that building maintenance all over the state had been postponed and postponed again, until, when the drought eased and we finally got rain, all the roofs leaked. The worst leak in our hall was in the foreign language lab, next door to my office. Our sole professor of foreign languages (French and German) was used to being passed over or forgotten, and he had long been making do with reel-to-reel tapes and phonograph records in an age of cassettes, and so in the midst of puddles and rivulets he had looked around for ways

to keep the lab more or less habitable and hit on the idea of setting houseplants under the drips. His largest container, under
the worst drip, was an old toilet, mint green, with a split-leaf
philodendron growing in its bowl.

The green toilet, when it first appeared, had stirred wry joking
among faculty and students—"I guess we know now that the
place is going down the toilet," etc.—but as time went on, other
topics took over, and I think we all stopped seeing the toilet.
My own reaction, when I would drop into the lab to visit, was
to note how well the philodendron was doing.

But now—"I'll get him!" gritted Studly. "You'll see that I will!"

My astonishment must have been written all over my face,
because he glared at me and flung out the door.

I sat alone, trying to make sense of his behavior. If I had learned
anything in my years as a dean, it was about the limitations of
power. The foreign language professor was fully tenured. Studly
couldn't "get" him for growing a philodendron in a green toilet
under a leak in the ceiling of the foreign language lab. Studly
could make an issue of the toilet, but why? It wasn't as though
the green toilet was in public view; we were lucky to have fifteen
or twenty students enrolled in foreign languages at any one time,
and those students would certainly side with the professor in
any toilet war.

And why was Studly so angry? I thought I had never seen
an administrator so enraged. Our little group tended toward
what a pop psychologist might have called passive-aggressive;
the dean of students, for instance, had ruled the campus with
an iron grip but was fond of talking about "warm fuzzies" and
"bluebird moments."

The dean of students was in trouble, though. First on Studly's
agenda when he arrived on campus was to destroy her. The
dean of students had fought back, but she stood no chance

against him; unlike the professor of foreign languages, she was untenured and served at the president's pleasure, and anyway her power base was melting away as her friends found jobs on other campuses. One day Studly called us all together to announce that the dean of students was retiring. Everyone stared at her. She smiled gallantly.

It was some time before I realized I was the one being threatened over the green toilet episode. Studly might not be able to "get" the foreign language professor, but he could "get" the dean.

But how could I think about Studly, when *never again* was what I thought about most days. Never again with my husband, whom I had loved. Never again the charge in the blood, never again the thrill in the loins, never again the sweet perverse certainty that anything is possible, to be desired, pursued, fucked, loved, kept. Never again the sensation of floating over the pavement, sunblind with the precious secret: *yes, yes, yes, he wants me!*

MY BODY WAS betraying me. Its first attack was a claw of pain through my shoulders. I couldn't turn my head without tears. Next came a gradual stiffening of my right arm. Within a week I couldn't reach behind my back to zip my skirt, and I took to getting dressed backward, zipping and buttoning my clothes in front and then twisting them into place. Probably arthritis, someone told me, and nothing to be done except learn to live with it. But my increasing, aching rigidity terrified me. It was as though I were turning to stone. I made an appointment with an orthopedic surgeon, who said I was probably headed for surgery on my rotator cuff. Otherwise, he remarked, I'd soon need someone to wipe my butt for me. I fled his office.

But I needed both my arms. I had Rachel to lug around, and I was dragging suitcases on and off airplanes on interviewing trips I was trying to keep secret. Who would want to hire a frozen woman with a face full of anguish? I experimented, rotating my shoulder into the pain until I could feel the bones grind, and I gritted my teeth and kept rotating, and eventually my arm worked, after a fashion.

WHEN THE BODY SHUTS down, feelings shut down. At first she regrets the loss of feelings. Never again to yearn for the dark male other? Never again to feel desire? But her regret fades with her other feelings, and so she makes her way through her days. Still, she has her child, and she has the work that supports the child. She never quite finishes anything; she never quite stretches the hours and minutes to cover the essentials. She has no energy for romance, no time for love, no strength left for rescuing her husband. So the thread is dropped, the labyrinth unexplored, the beast left unfed and alone at the heart of the conundrum.

DOWNSTAIRS, STUDLY PACES behind his glass doors. How his chest swells with dangerous energy! How he fumes at the state legislators whose powers exceed his! The tedious small-town straitjacket! What are his deep thoughts? All through the hallways, across the lawns in the far-flung buildings where classes are taught in diesel technology and farm–ranch management with feed, grain, and elevator options, the professors feel his dark vibrations and wonder what he's up to. They sense the charm of the man, the danger of the man as he prowls the corridor between his office and the secretarial workstations, glaring out at passing students or faculty or staff. Does he dream of a way back through the tortuous paths that have trapped him in this remote prairie outpost?

I HAD NEVER BEEN one of the dean of students' cronies—I had too recently been one of the faculty for her to trust me—but

Studly began to treat me as though I had been a member of her inner circle. I and such administrators who had not already resigned were increasingly isolated, given little work, left out of meetings and finding out about important decisions only when we overheard the faculty gossiping about them. One day, after a professor of science complained to Studly about a policy of President Erickson's that in point of fact I had protested at the time, Studly called me down to his office.

He glared at me as he laid out the new policy, gritted his words through his teeth. "That's how it's going to be. Have you got that loud and clear?"

"Yes," I said, too surprised to defend myself or ask for an explanation.

"Good!" He stood, dismissing me.

This clenched-teeth rage, unlike his real rage over the green toilet, had been a pose. I knew that. But why? We were alone in his office. He had no audience but me, and he knew I had no real power, so why the display?

Years later in retrospect, I realized the answer to that question. Because he, too, had so little real power, and because he could.

RELUCTANTLY I HAD BROUGHT myself to apply for positions in other states. Administrative positions, teaching positions, whatever I felt remotely qualified for. It was a wrenching process. After so many years of working in isolation on the Highline, I did not at heart believe any other institution would really want to hire me. Also, for all its poverty and isolation, I loved Northern Montana College. I loved my staunch, loyal secretary and I loved my second-floor office with its view of the huge western sky where thunderheads rolled across the endless blue and sunlight broke in shafts through storms. I loved my house on a residential hill, where a huge weeping birch shaded the front lawn and a diamond willow hung over the patio in back, where I played with Rachel and planted lilac twigs that I had thought to see bloom.

Meanwhile, tap tap tap went the sound of Bob's cowboy boots, to the rhythm of his feverish breathing, down the granite corridor outside my office. He was still haunting the place, still looking for my lover. Once I chanced a glimpse and saw that he had gone through the door into the English department, cornered a bewildered young professor, and was questioning him. I shrank back into my own office and sat with my head in my hands.

The world is small, and twenty-five years later, in another state, I will sit in the comfortable, cluttered campus office of a friend who had taught at Northern during the presidency of Studly, and my friend will tell me how that young professor and his wife began to be awakened by phone calls at two or three in the morning, the voice of the dean's husband on the line. *Where is she? I know she's with you! How is it with her? Is she enjoying it?*

In the myth we all remember, the girl gives the thread to the adventurer, who draws it through the labyrinth to the dark heart where the beast waits. The adventurer kills the beast, follows the thread back safely through the labyrinth, then abandons the girl.

But what if the girl drops the thread, what if she doesn't wait for the adventurer, what if she hardens her heart against adventurer and beast alike? I had loved Bob, but never again would I slide into bed with him, slide into the curve of his back, to feel his arm raised in drowsiness for me to slip my arm under his and fit myself to him and drift to sleep in his warmth and the faint sweet odor of his skin, the softness of his skin over muscle. Grieving, I survived only as my senses turned to stone.

Bob was trying to track me, to uncover my plans. He couldn't know where I was headed when I flew out of our small airport, but by driving around the parking lot he could see my car and know I was out of town. Late one night, back from a job interview and staggering out of the terminal with my suitcase, I was met by my secretary and her friend and her friend's husband.

"Don't try to start your car until we've checked it out! He hired a tow truck and has been towing it around town!"

The friend's husband looked under the hood. They he lay down on his back and squirmed under the car. Squirmed out again, shaking his head. Nothing was out of place, and I drove home and went to bed.

My most frightening symptom was my racing heart. I might be sitting at my desk, I might be thinking of nothing more stimulating than indirect cost ratios, when my heart would lurch and thunder into a pulse too rapid to count. I tried ignoring my heart, I tried working through its racehorse episodes, but I couldn't breathe, I couldn't concentrate. The only thing was lie down flat on my back behind my desk and wait until, in four or five minutes, my heart would give another lurch and resume its regular pace. One day I lay down behind my desk and my heart kept racing. My secretary fetched the professor of foreign languages from his watery lab, and he felt my pulse.

"I think you should go to the emergency room and get it checked out," he said in an unnaturally calm voice. He and my secretary helped me with my coat and drove me the few blocks to the hospital, where I was sedated for the night. Rachel went home with my secretary, and in the morning I was sent home with a prescription I have taken ever since.

I got my first inkling from the director of development, whom I met on the steps one morning.

"It's getting to be embarrassing," he said, "to have to go

downtown to talk about fundraising, and being asked, *What's going on in the president's office?*"

The pretty blonde wife was moving out of the presidential mansion. She was leaving the state. She was his third wife—fourth—*fifth*? The count grew as the gossip escalated. But wait! There was more.

Studly called a rare staff meeting to tell us how he had testified at a state legislative committee meeting and how well he had been received. We gathered in the student union ballroom, where the chairs had been arranged in a semicircle and coffee and cookies laid out on a side table. Studly seemed supercharged, chest expanding, necktie like a flag, almost dancing on his toes. He must have had a fine time down at the state capitol. He loved visiting the legislature. He was at his best before such audiences: handsome and articulate, displaying his trademark self-deprecating humor, charming even the most gnarled and conservative state senators. Now he was supervising the trays of cookies, stealing a cookie with that familiar self-deprecating gleam, oh naughty boy! And then I saw where his gaze was going, and I turned, and there was the young woman who coached the girls' volleyball team, suffused with color and helpless laughter from the heat of his eyes.

"Why?" the blonde wife was said to have asked. "Why are you leaving me for her?"

"Because you're beautiful," Studly was said to have answered, "and when we walk into a room, people look at you instead of me. With her, everyone will look at me."

The volleyball coach was plump, with close-set eyes and high cheekbones. Where she once had gone around campus in jeans and sweatshirts, she now favored tailored suits that looked a bit too old for her.

Said to have, said to have. As the gossip fueled itself, perhaps it also fueled Studly.

"This is too small a town," Studly was said to have said, "for my lifestyle."

WE WERE MIDWAY INTO the second year of Studly's presidency when my secretary told me he wanted to talk to me. She called down and made an appointment, and I dragged myself downstairs and through the glass doors. I knew what was going to happen. In his office sat Studly, all smiles. He had called me down to tell me that he had decided to terminate all the deans. My appointment would end on June 30.

He leaned forward across his desk, gleaming cuffs shot and hands clasped. I could see the tight pores of his fresh-shaven bronze face and the scar of his mended septum under his moustache. A birth defect, I wondered idly, or a later injury.

"You understand that I have to show the state legislature how deeply their budget cuts are going to affect us. But—I don't want you riding off into the sunset. I'll have a little something for you in the fall."

He winked at me.

I stared at him. What did a *wink* mean? Did he suppose I would trust his *wink*? I remembered the dean of students and her gallant smile, so I lifted my chin.

"I'll probably leave," I said, "but I do appreciate your consideration."

As it turned out, Studly fired nearly every administrator on campus that day, saving only himself, the current vice president, and one or two others. Comparing notes later, we learned that everyone had gotten a wink.

IN THEIR EFFORTS TO cut costs, the state legislators had decided to lower the number of service years that professors needed to retire. That way, they could get rid of more of us. I had been teaching since I was twenty. I counted up my years and months and discovered that, on June 30, I would lack about three weeks to qualify for retirement and a pension.

"I could stay through the fall semester and teach," I told the current vice president, reminding him that I still had faculty tenure, "but you'd have to fire a young professor to make room for me. Or you could give me a three-week contract to do whatever work needs to be done so I could be on my way."

"We'll do it," he said. "Don't worry."

Ten years earlier, before I became a dean and stopped writing fiction, I had published a book of short stories called *Lambing Out* (containing, of course, the short story I had written in graduate school, "Lambing Out," that had won the contest that had paid for my electric typewriter) with a university press. I hadn't expected my book to bring me fame and fortune, I wasn't that silly, but I did think it might make some kind of difference in my life. It did not. *Lambing Out* was the proverbial stone dropped into a pond with a sound or a ripple.

But searching *The Chronicle of Higher Education* for a job advertisement, any job advertisement, I came across a notice that Lewis-Clark State College in Idaho wanted to hire an assistant professor with a specialty in Shakespeare.

"While I understand that the position you advertise is a junior one, please know that I am seriously interested," I began my letter, and enclosed my vita with its description of my graduate seminars in Shakespeare, my long-ago dissertation on Ben Jonson, and, of course, *Lambing Out*.

Within a week, Dean Hugh Nichols of Lewis-Clark State College was on the phone. "The reason we're so interested in your candidacy is that you write fiction. We need somebody to teach the Shakespeare class, but we also want to develop a creative writing program, so you'd be just the person. Could we get you out to Idaho for an interview?"

I agreed to the interview and hung up the phone, feeling dazed at the irony. After all these years, it was the fiction that was going to save me.

But June came, and no three-week contract.

DON'T WORRY, the vice president had said, but I worried as I put my house up for sale. I had no illusions about the vice president's word or Studly's word, or his *wink*. I called Hugh Nichols, and he said they still wanted me and that they would let me start in January if I had to stay and teach through the fall semester. But, oh, how the professors in our English department would hate me, how I would hate myself for forcing out a young assistant professor.

Alternatively, I lectured myself. I was *selfish* for caring about a pension, *selfish* when I was able-bodied and employed, *worse* than selfish when I was getting ready to leave a terminally ill man and take his child when, after all, he hadn't been *physically* violent, not yet. Wouldn't I be nobler to make a sacrifice of myself and just go?

At last, shaken but unable to talk myself out of my own best interests, I called Studly.

He just laughed.

"So I can either stay through the fall semester—or leave."

"You got it," he said, and laughed again.

I cried for a while, picturing Studly behind his desk with his cuffs shot and his moustache almost hiding the faint scar under his nose while the light of the northern prairie fell through his windows and whitened his outline. I imagined how his face would be glowing with the pleasure of telling me, *you got it*.

Now he would be pushing back from his desk to pace the

twelve-by-twelve feet of his domain, perhaps to stroke the head of the bronze cowboy he had inherited from President Erickson, perhaps to gaze out at the view of hilltop and sky.

I remembered a time when Studly had asked me along with him to the state capitol to testify before some committee, and the pretty blonde wife decided to come with us. I remembered sitting alone in the back seat on the way home while the president and his wife fell into a private conversation. There might have been a thunderstorm purpling over the prairie that evening, or perhaps only a spectacular shift in the light as the sun sank. The peaks of a low mountain range would have risen in the distance, the wind would have ruffled the miles of native grass and sagebrush.

"We wouldn't have seen anything like this if I'd taken the Pennsylvania job," Studly had remarked to the wife who sat beside him in her prim pastel suit.

Those were my mountains, that was my sky. I had lived within this landscape most of my professional life. I stopped crying and thought about my options. I knew a local state senator who, for cloudy political reasons, hated Studly. I picked up the telephone and dialed.

"Let me make a call or two," said the senator, after he listened to my story.

Half an hour later, my phone rang. It was Studly. "I *misunderstood* you," he said. "Of course we'll have a contract for you. It'll be in my office tomorrow, ready to sign."

BEING A DEAN HAD meant better pay, but it also had been the end of my aspirations to be a writer. Now, at Lewis-Clark State College, I was a professor again. Safe from Studly, safe from Bob, but with an uneasy tendency to watch my back, I dropped off Rachel at the college's day care and taught my classes in writing and literature and began to write again, as the words and sentences and paragraphs that had eluded the dean began to return to the teacher. Studly had inadvertently done me a great favor. If he hadn't fired me, I might have gone on being a dean forever.

Time passed. After I fled with Rachel, Bob lived for another two years, hobbling about with a portable oxygen tank and cursing his ill fortune, but we never saw him again. He died alone and enraged and trapped in his own tightening prison by disease and circumstance. Rachel began school and moved from one grade to the next, and I went on teaching and writing. Eventually the chairman of the English department at the University of Idaho invited me to join his faculty and help to start an MFA program in creative writing, and so Rachel and I moved up to Moscow, Idaho, where I have lived and taught ever since.

And yet the world is small, and I hadn't heard the last of Studly. I knew when he left impoverished little Northern for the presidency of another, wealthier, more prestigious campus, and I imagined him ascending his ladder into the rarified clouds of higher education with his glossy cuffs, his sun-bronzed face, his buffed image and, yes, the girls' volleyball coach.

I have never gotten over my dean's habit of reading *The Chronicle of Higher Education*. Twenty years after I left Northern, I came upon an article describing a controversy at a distant university. A famous writer had been invited by students at that university to discuss a book she had written about political responsibility. The president of the university, however, on hearing whom the students had invited, insisted that she sign a pledge that nothing she would say would embarrass the Republican governor of the state. The writer refused. She returned the students' speaking fee and gave her talk, gratis, across the street from the campus.

I was acquainted with the writer, and I thought of getting in touch with her, telling her how much I admired her graciousness and telling her my own story. But time passed, and anyway, what was my story really about?

But then an old friend from Havre sent me a photocopy of an article from a distant newspaper, along with a note: *We're all buzzing about this. We thought you'd want to know.*

I skimmed the article, then reread it. The president of that distant university, the same man who had been featured in the *Chronicle* article, the man who had told me, *you got it*, had just been forced to retire because of his affair with a female professor. Her name meant nothing to me, and I wondered what had become of the girls' volleyball coach as I read the charges listed in the newspaper article: that the president had bypassed university policy to fund a program for his mistress to teach in, that he had used his influence to get her unfavorable teacher evaluations erased, that he had fired several deans in retaliation for their opposition.

So that was what had become of the adventurer.

I told myself that he finally didn't matter, not to me and not to the writer who had defied him and had the courage to speak across the street from his campus to the students who had invited her. But this time—and I asked myself, why, for the pleasure of passing gossip, or out of vindictiveness?—I did send her an email and almost immediately I got back a long and anguished reply which ended, *I look back now and he seems either like a bad joke or a bad dream.*

Whose bad joke, whose bad dream? All stories deserve conclusions, even if life doesn't always supply them. One version of the story about the girl who gave the thread to the adventurer tells that he abandoned her, pregnant, to die in childbirth; another version tells that he took her away with him, only to see her murdered by an angry goddess; still another version tells that the abandoned girl was rescued by a god, who gave her a crown of stars. I didn't die, and the only stars I saw were from my two husbands' parting blows, but I did drop the thread and go my own way, telling myself *never again, never again.*

10

1960

A WINTER EVENING IN Missoula, Montana. Snow blows against
the blackened window behind Dr. Leslie Fiedler, who sits at
the head of a conference table in one of the smaller classrooms
in the liberal arts building at the University of Montana. Ten
or twelve of us are gathered around the table, listening as Dr.
Fiedler reads aloud my short story, "Custis for Us at the U."
My story is about a high school football star who doesn't want
to go to college but is being pressured to accept a scholarship.
Dr. Fiedler reads very well. He is a thickset bearded man with
a mane of dark hair and pale, penetrating eyes that rise often
from the page to scan our faces. Many of the citizens of western
Montana believe he is evil—he is liberal, urban, and Jewish, after
all—but I'm only nineteen and I don't understand why it's evil

to be liberal or what it means when he's attacked in letters to the student newspaper for being an existentialist. I live for his word of praise.

I have taken previous creative writing classes (I have never heard them called workshops) from several professors here at the university. The famous Walter Van Tilburg Clark had left Missoula for Reno, Nevada, before I ever arrived, but he left his mark on the program, and we creative writing students have been assigned "The Portable Phonograph" and "Indian Well" again and again. There was Robert O. Bowen, who had written several novels and taught my freshman honors class but left Montana in some kind of huff, and there was bluff, elderly Henry V. Larom, who had written a series of young adult mysteries known as the Mountain Pony books. Dr. Seymour Betsky taught the evening creative writing class at least once, and so did a youngish man I remember only because he remarked that Katherine Anne Porter's story "The Grave" wasn't much good, being about birth and such, of interest only to women.

Now, however, the evening creative writing classes seem to belong to Dr. Fiedler. Many years later I will suspect the various waves and shifts over creative writing were symptoms of something seismic in that English department. It was an English department, after all, and an English department that, in a few years, would hire a poet named Richard Hugo and inaugurate a then-unheard-of MFA degree in creative writing. But in 1960 I am unsuspicious and uninformed and interested only in Dr. Fiedler's opinion of my short story.

That he's reading my work aloud is a sign of the times. We have a copy center on campus where we can leave off typescript to be duplicated and picked up the next day, but the usual procedure in the creative writing classes is for the students to give their stories to the instructor, who selects the pieces he wants to read aloud during the weekly class meeting. We are expected to listen and comment on each other's work, based on what we've just heard and can recall. Previous instructors have given us a few rules for writing fiction. (Dr. Fiedler isn't much for laying down rules for writing.) The first line of a story, we've been taught, should state the theme of the story as a whole, although not in so many words. A story's conclusion should contain a moment of revelation; if it doesn't, it's not a story but a sketch. Also, a story's viewpoint should never shift. We all listen vigilantly for shifting points of view in each other's work.

My story ends with my football star, finding no way out of his dilemma, running through the streets of his hometown with no goal in sight. Dr. Fiedler reads the final sentence and lays the typed sheets on the table in front of him. Looks around the table and waits.

Most of the students who look back at him are young men, who may reflect the campus ratio of men to women more than they indicate a male interest in writing. These men have read Hemingway and understand that stories should be about violent death or life in the military, or they've read Kerouac and understand that stories should be about gifted artists who have no money but travel a lot, smoke a lot, and drink lot of wine. Another sign of our times is that there's no explicit sex and few obscenities in theirs or any other stories, although there are plenty of thwarted relationships followed by despair.

"I just thought it was a boring story," says the large young man sitting next to Dr. Fiedler. "I couldn't get interested in—what was his name?"

A sophomore, daughter of a well-known Montana writer, suggests that the minor characters in the story are stereotypes.

"I just feel like I've read it before, somewhere," says another student, raising her eyebrows and sighing, as though to imply that the story, with its boring stereotypical characters, has been plagiarized.

"Did the point of view shift? I can't remember," says somebody else.

Other opinions rise around the table, few favorable. We tend not to like each other's work, although there are a few alliances and separate conversations among students who have shared previous classes, like my friend Marcy Melton, who like me is married and lives off campus. Marcy writes wonderful stories about long silences between husbands and wives, which I listen to with bitter envy. But tonight I wait through the discussion for the only opinion that matters. Finally Dr. Fiedler picks up the sheets of my story and shuffles them back into a stack. "The interesting thing," he says, "is that, at the end, the main character falls back on the one thing he's good at, which is running."

Is this praise? I can't be certain; it's impossible to be certain what Dr. Fiedler is thinking, or what he perceives when he scans our faces with those pale eyes. I'm terrified of him, of course. I can hardly bring myself to speak in his presence. But—*the interesting thing*—at least he's not condemning my story, at least he's read it, and he's found something worthy of comment in it. If this is not praise, at least it's enough for me to live on and write until time for class next week.

1988

AN EARLY SPRING EVENING in Lewiston, Idaho, where I came to live last fall and teach at Lewis-Clark State College. The town of Lewiston stretches itself along the confluence of the Clearwater and Snake rivers, sheltered by the great gray river bluffs and blessed by a mild climate that allows magnolias and dogwoods to blossom in the shadow of the Rocky Mountains. On campus the pink and white petals float down to the lawns and flowerbeds while water sprinklers swish in the gathering darkness. The lushness unsettles me as I walk across the campus, still wearing one of my dean's suits and high-heeled shoes. After eighteen years of living in Havre, on northern Montana's gray prairie, I can't get used to the softness of the weather or the profusion of roses here, or the meticulous way this campus is maintained, as though I've found myself living in unearned luxury. *They actually patch the leaks in the roofs here? What a concept!*

It's not that Lewis-Clark State College or its faculty and staff have had it easy. The college began as the state normal school, to train teachers. In the 1960s, during the throes of a financial crisis in Idaho, the legislature actually closed the college, which stood empty and deteriorating while ivy grew through the windows of Spalding Hall, where the English department offices currently are located. Opening its doors again to students in the 1970s, the college gradually found a new niche for itself, not only in its wide range of vocational and technical programs, but as a doorway for the so-called nontraditional student. In 1988 the average age for a student here is about thirty-three, and all the professors have gotten used to seeing graying, timorous heads among the eighteen-year-olds.

Last Chance State College, its detractors call this college, but in the short time I've taught here, I've come to realize that the nickname is accurate, although not in the way it's intended. A last chance, yes, for the divorced woman with children to support, who writes painfully that she knows an education is the only way she'll ever get herself and the kids out of that basement apartment and on their way. A last chance in a different way for the retired man of fixed income who tells me that the college library and college classrooms offer him the least expensive and most stimulating experience of his life.

A last chance, for that matter, for me.

Last fall—my first semester at Lewis-Clark—I taught a class of freshman composition that was comprised of eighteen-year-olds along with several women in their late thirties who had taken time off from their jobs at a local ammunition factory to see whether, as one put it, "I could *do* college-level work." These women watched their young classmates stumble in, late and bleary-eyed and hungover from their weekends. They shook their heads at the excuses they heard for missing essays, at the lame answers, at the resistance to the reading assignments.

"Now that I know I can do college-level work, I don't know whether I'll do any more of it," one of these women told me at the end of the semester. Then she added, "One thing I learned for sure this semester. I'll never try to get one of my kids to start college before he wants to go!"

I LEARNED TO TEACH freshman composition by trial and error years ago, under the benevolent rule of Willoughby Johnson at the University of Missouri, and I'm fine with those classes and also with the survey of British literature and the Shakespeare class I've been assigned. But this evening I'm meeting a class in the writing of creative nonfiction, and it's a new venture for me as well as for the eighteen students who have arranged themselves in a loose circle, waiting to begin. My only guide to teaching creative writing, let alone this new genre of creative nonfiction that seems to have sprung up overnight, is what I can remember from Dr. Fiedler's long-ago evening classes. Should I read somebody's work aloud and see what the students say about it?

About half of the students in our circle are what we've come to call "traditional." That is, they started college right out of high school and now, as juniors or seniors, are in their late teens or early twenties. Two or three others are local schoolteachers, perhaps picking up recertification credits. But a sizeable group can charitably be called "older," if not downright elderly. Most are women, with one or two men, all white haired and favoring the forgiving shapelessness of polyester slacks and sweatshirts. What they hope, as I have discovered, is to rescue their childhoods.

Just as I once studied books on theater and stagecraft, I've searched through my stack of writing craft books, sent to me by publishers who hope I will require my students to buy them. I've found plenty of advice at the self-help level for writing poetry or fiction or even drama, but hardly anything on this new genre that is getting plenty of fun poked at it—defined by what it is not, etc.—but little that will help the traditional students get started, or the schoolteachers get grades of A, or the older folks relive the past. So I've borrowed and patched pieces of advice where I can, and one of my borrowings tells students to note on each other's work anything they don't understand.

Tonight we're discussing a draft written by a student who probably is in her seventies. She has told us that she spent her childhood in a lumber camp near Pierce, Idaho, a place with no resonance for me, but whose mention makes all the older students smile and shake their heads. Unlike me and my snotty little fellow students at the University of Montana, these people tend to love each other's work.

"We used to get real snow in Pierce, snow like you never see nowadays! The snow would get so deep that the path my father shoveled from the kitchen door to the outhouse would eventually get to be a tunnel, and we would be glad of that tunnel all winter long," she has written.

Her friends nod their heads in corroboration of the snow depth of years past, and one or two raise their hands and contribute anecdotes of their own.

The writer continues. "My mother would wash our clothes

and hang them outside to freeze-dry on the line. Then she would bring them inside, sprinkle them, and iron them."

There's a pause. A twenty-year-old studies his copy of her draft (we've progressed at least to the point of having copies of each other's work for everyone to read ahead of time). He raises his hand. "You told us to mark anything we didn't understand. What exactly did her mother do to the clothes? *Sprinkle*? What's that?"

In the silence, as the old folks exchange startled looks, I have a flash of all the time that has passed for them and also for me. How can I ever tell the story of my own life, even to my own children?

THE NEXT MORNING, in Spalding Hall, I join the little group standing around the main office and tell the story of the young man who didn't know what it meant to sprinkle clothes. The department secretary laughs.

"I grew up in Illinois," she says, "and the weather in summer was so humid that the sprinkled clothes would mildew overnight, so my mother would roll them in towels and put them in the refrigerator. We all got used to seeing those long ropy rolls of laundry whenever we went for a soda."

"My mother would put a perforated cap on a pop bottle and fill it with water to sprinkle the clothes," says somebody else.

Hearing their stories, I don't feel quite as antiquated as I did last night. And through the witchcraft of association, I'm seeing the flash of my mother's hand, dipped in water (she wouldn't have bothered with filling a pop bottle and shaking it) to dash over her dry clothes before she bundles them into a bath towel. Then the odor of burning wood, flatirons heating on the stove, and a shape, like a mist rising over the ironing board from the starch and the steam, or a materialization of this strange genre of creative nonfiction.

So that's what the genre is for. Now, if I can just figure out how to teach the craft.

2010

I'M STILL TRYING to figure it out (although at least I no longer wear suits and high heels to class, but have graduated back to the blue jeans of my girlhood). The University of Idaho is not the Ivy League, but still, I felt intimidated when I first moved "up the hill," as they say in Lewiston, to help inaugurate the MFA program in creative writing. One of the graduate students in the first creative nonfiction class I taught at the University of Idaho wrote in an evaluation, *I don't think she knows a thing about rhetoric or composition theory.* The student was right. I've tried to read some of the theory, but it seems as arcane as Jacques Derrida's *différance* or *aporia*, less grounded than nursing theory, and I grasp it only by translating it into story as I go along. My impression—maybe my illusion—is that the rhetoricians live by precepts that guide their writing through a more rigorous and orderly process than my fumbling for images.

Do rhetoricians feel pain? I've often wondered. *I felt a little gross writing about something so painful for my family,* writes one of my current graduate students. *Plumbing for my parents' reaction, running to my room to copy snatches of dialogue. What an asshole I am. Is that what nonfiction writers are made to do?*

All I can tell her is how I feel when I write about a dead husband, or about a still-living ex-husband whose follies, forty years ago, were no worse than my own.

Our MFA program is strong and competitive, and we've managed to maintain its integrity even as higher education in Idaho is battered by our current financial crisis (how many more, Lord, how many more). Our students submit their work for publication, and some of it is accepted, and some of our graduates have gone on to good tenure-track jobs, teaching writing. In workshops these days we look up from our perusal of each other's drafts to discuss the current questions: whether it is important to keep to factual truth in creative nonfiction or whether, as some well-known writers insist, it's more important to present "emotional truth." Students worry about the pundits who warn that memoir writing is lazy writing and advise that they ought to be writing fiction. I think about my experience with Mrs. Skaarda, so long ago, and the fiction I made of it, and I wonder why fiction is thought to plumb more "truth" than nonfiction does, when in either genre it's the witchcraft of association and the projection of imagination that opens doorway after doorway in the haunted labyrinth that folds and unfolds and never comes to an end.

So many voices to tell us what we ought not to write.

To write about other people is a betrayal.

To write about yourself is navel-gazing.

Discussions of craft are more sophisticated than ever before. We talk about focus and narrative arc. We consider linear and nonlinear structures. When we discuss shifting points of view, it's to decide whether to shift and why. Moments of revelation? The term seems dated, and I remember a recent graduate student in fiction, after reading several writers' low opinions of epiphanies, coming to class with her draft and saying, "I'm afraid I've got one."

I'm more fluent than I once was in the terminology of craft, and I when I leave a literature class to teach a creative writing class, I don't feel the old awkward panic, as though I'm in one of those dreams where I've agreed to perform in grand opera and find myself on stage, naked, without being able to sing a note.

But when I remember those classes that Dr. Fiedler presided over, I remember those pale eyes scanning us with a hint of withheld amusement. What did he know that we didn't? That however sophisticated the workshop discussion, what matters is the day-in, day-out work, the writing to meet the deadline, the presentation to the audience. The one or two words of praise to live on for the next week.

The lonely walk home to start rewriting.

Epilogue

HERE IN MOSCOW a windstorm tore through the trees during the night and littered my deck with broken branches, twigs, decapitated cottonwood leaves, and tatters of long narrow willow leaves. Before the leaves could wilt, before I could sweep up and trash the branches, Rachel's eleven-month-old daughter, Cali, toddled out into the clean morning and saw that her familiar deck was now a strange green garden.

She picked up a leafy branch, waved it, then used it to switch the cat until, annoyed, the cat leaped to the deck rail to sit out of her reach with his tail tucked around him. I watched as Cali's eyes followed the cat and then wandered above and beyond him into the quivering green canopy between her and the leftover shreds of clouds. As though she had just realized where her branch had been torn from, she stretched it up toward the tree as high as she could, offering it with all the voice she had:

"Ohh! Ohh!"

And I imagined the thought she was trying to articulate: *Tree! Don't you want your branch back?*

I think I must have lost my own wonder at a cat's agility or a branch torn from a tree when I was quite young, because I remember spending quite a bit of my childhood being bored on that isolated cattle ranch in Montana, confined by boring old hills of sagebrush and shale, a drab blue arch of sky, and dust that blew across the road to elsewhere. Elsewhere was where I wanted to be, where the adventures I read about in books were happening without me. Oh, I was so bored! I had read every one of my books again and again, and my only playmate, my little sister, was taking her nap. If only I had something to do! If only I were an Indian child, like Bear Paw and Bright Star, who led such interesting lives, tanning hides and chipping arrowheads, in *Our Little Neighbors at Work and Play*.

But wait! There was an idea!

And so, at age seven, I began manufacturing bows and arrows. Using *Our Little Neighbors at Work and Play* as a kind of instruction manual, with a paring knife stolen from my mother's kitchen, I carved the bows out of willow branches and strung them with the heavy white "store string" that in those days came around packages of groceries or hardware or anything else purchased in town. My arrows were unfletched willow twigs, notched on one end and blunt on the other (although I tried, with gravel picked up from the road, I never figured out how to chip an arrowhead), and they were bumpy and erratic, but satisfyingly lofty in flight.

Now all I needed was a target. As the thought came to me, I noticed my rancher grandmother trudging up from the barn with a bucket of chicken feed in either hand, and I drew back my bow and loosed my wobbling, knobbled arrow, and hit her, dead center.

She dropped her buckets. I tell myself now that I couldn't have hurt her, not with a blunt willow twig perhaps a half inch in diameter and fourteen inches long, but I must have startled the hell out of her, and I decided that some distance between us would be no bad thing, so I retreated to the other side of the ash pile and waited, on the balls of my bare feet, as my grandmother picked up the bow and arrow I had dropped. It was clear that she intended to shoot me with it, and equally clear that she didn't have the hang of the mechanism. Fascinated, I watched as she drew the bow backwards, nocked the arrow, and shot herself with it.

My father, coming out of the barn on some errand, saw it all. When he doubled over with laughter, my grandmother turned on him so wrathfully that she forgot, for the moment, about me.

My rancher grandmother had been a schoolteacher in Philadelphia before journeying to Montana to live with an uncle and teach in a one-room school the uncle had started. Then she married her first cousin, my grandfather, who had stopped cowboying and begun ranching on the south slopes of the South Moccasin Mountains, the same slopes under the same sky I later found so boring. My father was only three years old when my grandfather died, and my grandmother, more or less single-handedly, kept the ranch running until my father was old enough to take over.

By the time I was old enough to remember her (and, God knows, shoot her with a bow and arrow), she was deeply tanned and seamed, with white hair she kept scraped back in a tight bun until the work of the day loosened the strands to hang in her face. In my mind's eye I see her in flickering snapshots. At branding time, she stands over her pitch-pine fire to tend the branding irons. Every chance she gets, she'll unroll her knitting from a clean dish towel and add a row or two before my father strides over to reach though the corral fence and swap a cold iron for a hot one. At fencing time, she pounds away with a crowbar at gravel and gumbo baked hard as clay, and then she scoops out the loosened soil with the two-handled posthole diggers. She'll have her posthole dug by the time my father gets back with a creosote-soaked post to set and string with barbed wire. At haying time, she drives the stacker team back and forth in the chaff and dust. Back and forth, back and forth, the big crossbred workhorses plod and she plods after them, while the haylift rises, drops its sweet load of curing hay on top of the stack, and settles again to receive another load from the teeth of my father's horse-drawn buck rake.

My rancher grandmother rounds up books for me, discards from around the family or outdated textbooks like *Our Little Neighbors at Work and Play*. I can never get my hands on enough books (hence my habit of reading again and again the ones I've got). When someone gives me *Little Women*, I'm ecstatic because I've heard so much about Meg and Jo and Beth and Amy from my teacher grandmother and also from my rancher grandmother. Absorbed, dazed, I read and read and then leave *Little Women* on the back step when I'm called to supper, and that night it rains.

"What were you thinking," screams my mother. "Your brand new book!"

But my rancher grandmother builds a fire in the wood stove, sets *Little Women* in the oven, and painstakingly dries it out, page by page, to be read twice, three times, ten times over before being shelved where it sits in a backstairs bookcase to this day, still a bit swollen from its long-ago soaking and its oven rescue.

She was a veteran storyteller. *One time—*

That was how she started the stories she told to keep me entertained as I followed along, barefoot, behind the stacker team, or hung around the branding fire, or watched her set fence posts.

One time when I was a little girl in Philadelphia, our milk cow got out of her pen and ran off down the lane, and my father sent me and my brother, Elias, to catch her. Elias and I ran after the cow, and the cow ran and ran, but finally I caught her by the tail and hung on. For some reason, that made the cow turn and run back to her pen, and I hung on and shut the gate behind us. Then up the lane came Elias, singing, Hanging on a cow's tail! Hanging on a cow's tail! My father looked at him and his singing and said, She got the cow back, didn't she. That shut him up.

Elias died young, you know. He had tuberculosis, and they thought if he came out to Montana to herd sheep, the dry air would help his lungs. But it rained hard that spring, and he died, and his was the first grave in the cemetery in Lewistown.

A story that didn't start with *one time*, that could be told only when none of the men were around, had to do with the birth of my father. The plan had been that my grandmother and her mother would make the eight-mile wagon journey from the ranch to the train station at Danvers (figure three or four miles an hour behind a team of workhorses), where they could take a train to Lewistown and stay with my grandfather's parents to await the baby's birth.

We were sitting in the kitchen of the old ranch house, and my mother was cutting sandwiches for the drive to Lewistown, when I felt something strange. I said, Mama, I feel like I've wet my pants! But I know I didn't wet my pants! She said, Oh, my goodness, your water broke, and she went right on cutting sandwiches. After awhile I said, Mama, are we still going to Lewistown? My goodness, no, she said, we won't have time now to get to Lewistown before the baby's born. I said, so Mama, why are you still cutting sandwiches?

The old two-storied ranch house was still standing when I was a child, a half mile up the creek from where we lived. Its log walls were still sound, and in summer the hollyhocks planted by my great-grandmother bloomed around the front door that faced the wagon road. My mother and grandmother kept various household overflow in the old ranch house, and sometimes in late summer we'd all walk up to retrieve boxes of glass jars for canning. We had to be careful, though, because rattlesnakes were likely to coil and nap in the hollyhocks and weeds, and back of the house the porch that overlooked the creek was sagging off its supports. (The story was that my father had once ridden his tricycle off that porch and fallen into the creek.) The old house always seemed spacious if shadowy to me, with its large kitchen and front room and its stairs to the bedrooms where I imagined ghosts creaked, and I used to wonder why we didn't still live there.

In one of those upstairs bedrooms, my father had been born; delivered, I suppose, by his grandmother, my great-grandmother Rachel.

THERE WERE EIGHT of us standing around the delivery room the day Cali was born. Rachel's ex-boyfriend, the father-to-be; his mother and sister; myself; and my older daughter, Elizabeth, and my foster daughter, Misty, each with a child of theirs in tow. Elizabeth's seven-year-old Ali and Misty's four-year-old Tayler were eager and agog at the prospect of a new cousin. The walls of the delivery room were brightly stenciled, and there was a playroom down the hall where we could take the little kids if they got bored. Rachel, cheerful after her epidural, lay on her gurney with her legs in the stirrups and watched a poker tournament on the raised television set. When the doctor arrived at the last minute (at least that feature of hospital birthing hadn't changed), he perched on his stool between Rachel's legs but kept glancing over his shoulder at the cards being dealt on the screen.

Rachel's ex-boyfriend held her hands and coached her through her contractions. "Okay, here we go again. One, two, three, push," as the rest of us watched the baby's crown seemingly stuck in place. Finally the doctor reached for a gadget that made me think of a plumber's helper and attached it to the crown. As Ali and Tayler jostled each other and dodged around his shoulders to get a better look, the doctor used his suction gadget to draw Cali slowly out into the bright light.

"She'll be a cone head for awhile," he said, "but it won't last long."

The ex-boyfriend was handed a pair of shears for the ritual cutting of the umbilical cord. A nurse scooped up Cali and carried her away to a heated table to sponge and dress her. Ali and Tayler hurried to watch, and soon Tayler rushed back to report, "She put a little cap on the baby's head!"

"She's perfect!" gasped Rachel, when she finally held Cali in her arms.

"Only way I deliver them," said the doctor, departing.

I thought of the birth of my first baby, how I had been given an enema and had my pubic hair shaved and then had been left alone to lie on my back with my increasing pains in a darkened room with nothing but the night sounds of a hospital between me and my fears. It was a night that seemed never to end. The dawn of a June morning finally broke through the high windows, and I was wheeled into the delivery room and given gas, which I gulped into oblivion and woke a little later to be handed a bundled baby with the deep marks of forceps on both sides of his tiny skull.

My father also was born in June, after a long labor. *I had such a hard time*, my grandmother told my mother, in the secretive voice the women used in those days to talk about birth or death or sex or violence, as though they were passing messages from some subversive parallel world, *that my husband didn't want me ever to have another.*

Given the choice, would she rather have made the two- or three-hour journey by wagon, bumping over ruts under a scorching prairie sun or huddling under a blanket while the horses churned and struggled through the mud of June rains? Then an hour's rumbling train ride? Would she rather have lain in an upstairs bedroom in her mother-in-law's house, knowing that a doctor could have been called to her side if her labor went wrong, that there was a hospital in Lewistown (indeed the same hospital where, fifty years later, I lay alone all night in labor) where she could have been carried if her labor went badly wrong?

She didn't have a choice. *It always rains on my birthday,* my father used to say, so maybe a window was open and my grandmother could hear rain falling on the eaves and through the grass and into the creek. Rain was so scanty in dry Montana that everybody prayed it would fall and fall, but perhaps my grandmother thought of the wagon ride in the rain and was thankful she at least had been spared that. She hadn't lived so long in Montana that the sound of rainfall had become music to her ears, or the distant bawling of a range cow for her calf as ordinary as the chattering of magpies in the cottonwood trees, not to a girl from Philadelphia, even from a part of Philadelphia so rural that the family kept a milk cow.

Downstairs her husband would have started a wood fire in the kitchen range, boiling water in kettles and sterilizing sheets in the oven. Her mother would have been in and out of her room, soothing her to sleep between pains, perhaps reading aloud to her, perhaps (after all, the storytelling impulse in our family came from somewhere) reassuring her with stories about the births of her own children, or stories she had heard from her mother or grandmother about the births of children in a dimmer past.

Her name was Rachel. Rachel Woodington. What little I know about her was told to me by my grandmother or my father, who loved her deeply. I am under the impression she came to Philadelphia from England. In Philadelphia she married a carpenter named Howard Hogeland. I still possess two straight-backed chairs with rush-bottom seats, said to have been crafted by Howard, and also a child's bentwood chair he made for his and Rachel's first child. The rush-bottom chairs are very fragile now, and they hold only the emptiness left by my rancher grandmother, but the little bentwood chair is sturdy. Cali often drags it out to sit on. It is just her size.

HER OTHER GRANDMOTHER, Martha, usually picks Cali up on Saturday afternoons to spend the night. Cali loves these visits. She is old enough now to run to the door, squealing and clapping her hands, when she hears the doorbell. Martha will scoop her up, along with her small pink suitcase, and Cali will bounce with anticipation.

"Bye," she will tell me, importantly. "Bye."

(And what of Cali's parents? Her father lives with a new girlfriend; he's said to be working construction; well, no, he either quit or got fired; I can't keep track of his life. Cali's mother, my Rachel, seemed to recover from the depression in her teens that hospitalized her for weeks in a locked ward under suicide watch. And yet Rachel lives in a haze that I can't penetrate or comprehend. Cali's lucky to have you, say my friends, and I say, yes, and lucky to have Martha, also.)

When she brings Cali home on Sunday afternoons, Martha and I often chat for a few minutes, a conversation of interest only to a pair of doting grandmothers. Cali's learning to say please and thank you, she can tell you what a dog says (ruff, ruff) and what a tiger says (grr, grr) and what a bee says (buzz, buzz), this afternoon she enjoyed running up and down the bleachers at her teenaged uncle's baseball game, yes, she's had a good dinner, yes, she should sleep well tonight.

"Bye," Cali tells her grandmother Martha. "Bye."

MY TWO GRANDMOTHERS WERE good friends. The one gnarled and scarred from years of ranching, the other a little more polished but equally battle hardened by her years of teaching in rural schools. On weekends my teacher grandmother often came to visit, and she and my rancher grandmother would sit by the oil heater in the cabin and knit and chat.

One time (*one time*, I might someday begin a story to Cali) my parents left my sister and me in the care of the two grandmothers and went off somewhere in the truck. It was a cold, stinging March in Montana, and the grandmothers were hunkered down by the oil heater, absorbed in whatever they were talking about. They failed to notice when I stole out the door in search of something to do, taking my little sister with me.

I was six, my sister three. What would be something interesting to do?

The irrigation ditch was running high and fast and cold from mountain snowmelt. I took off all my clothes and helped my sister take off her clothes, and we waded into a current that was thigh-high on me, waist-high on her. Debris from the mountains, bits of pine bark and pine needles, washed past us. My teeth were chattering and I couldn't see my feet through the muddy water, but I was enjoying the cushiony sensation of walking on an inch or two of mud at the bottom of the ditch, and I didn't notice when my sister crawled out of the water and fled.

"She was so cold she couldn't talk!" my teacher grandmother

later reported. "We heard something scratch at the door and went to look, and there she was! Poor little girl, she'd turned blue!"

I was squatting in the ditch, trying to feel the muddy bottom with my hands without getting ditchwater in my mouth, when I heard my rancher grandmother shout from the kitchen door. I watched her run the thirty yards to the ditch. Why was she in such a hurry? She grabbed me by one arm, hauled me out of the water, and set such a brisk pace back to the house that I had to trot to keep up.

They had to wait for buckets of water to heat on the coal range before they could bathe us, so my teacher grandmother stood my little sister on a chair, and my rancher grandmother stood me on a chair, and they toweled us down to the tune of *whatever possessed you* and *didn't you know you were cold* and *do you realize you could have drowned* while our teeth rattled in our heads. The point of the story, as they later told it to our parents, was that I had stayed in the freezing water after my little sister turned blue and fled for the house. They had had to drag me out.

MY RANCHER GRANDMOTHER used to keep by her a framed photograph of her mother, Rachel Woodington, holding my father in her arms when my father was about the age Cali is now (nearly two at the time I write). I have always loved the photograph, which I have inherited: the grave, sad-eyed woman in her formal dark dress, with her head inclined toward the little boy who leans against her. Could my father ever have been so light haired, so tender limbed in a white linen sailor suit?

"He loved her more than he loved me," my rancher grand-mother used to say.

"No wonder she loved him so much," my mother would say, "when she'd just lost her own boy."

As nearly as I can piece it together, Rachel left Philadelphia after the deaths of her husband and her son, Elias, and traveled out to Montana by train, a journey that would have taken several days but was a marvel of public convenience compared with the endless miles of highway in the American West to be traversed by automobile today. Rachel could have taken a direct sleeper from Philadelphia to Chicago, where she might have changed to the Great Northern line, which would have taken her to Havre, in northern Montana. My grandmother had a story about traveling by team and wagon from the ranch in central Montana up to Havre to meet someone's train, a journey of 180 miles that involved camping out several nights on the prairie. On one of those nights, the tent caught fire, nothing serious, but a scare nonetheless. Perhaps it was Rachel's train she and my grandfather were going to meet.

Once in Montana, Rachel filed on a homestead, which eventually would be absorbed into the family ranch, and she took over most of the care of my father after his father died and his mother took over the management of the ranch. Busy and absorbed, my rancher grandmother took to her work. I once read an essay my father wrote as an assignment for his correspondence school, in which he discussed the importance of the *Lewistown Democrat-News* for his mother as she tracked cattle prices. Meanwhile Rachel cooked and mended and kept house. My glimpses of her come from my father. How she used to pin her mending to the front of her dress to anchor it, and how, occasionally, she would set her tiny stitches all the way through to her dress and have to unstitch herself, and how annoyed she would be.

The main floor of the log house was heated by a wood stove in the kitchen and a stone fireplace in the other big room, but the bedrooms upstairs were frigid during Montana winters, when the temperature often plummeted to thirty or forty degrees below zero. I imagine the teeth-chattering little boy, his breath puffing white around his head, stripping down to his long johns and bundling under a mound of covers to watch the receding shadow of his grandmother, Rachel, as she carried away the kerosene lamp.

"As long as she was alive, I always went to bed with a hot water bottle," he told me. "After she died, I never had another hot water bottle."

Rachel died when my father was a senior in high school. Maybe his mother, my rancher grandmother, thought he was old enough to boil water and fill his own water bottle if he wanted one.

My rancher grandmother always slept with a hot water bottle herself, though. I know because I shared her bed until I was ten or so, and I well remember the hot water bottle, a rubbery orange container with a stopper, about the size of a bathroom scale. Placed under the covers at the foot of the bed, it not only warmed the sheets but exuded a dangerous heat when touched by a child's exploring toe. By morning it would have lost its power, reduced to a flaccid rubber bag of cold water that sloshed unpleasantly when disturbed.

A COUSIN RECENTLY SENT me, via the mysterious channels of wireless, two photos of Rachel that I had not seen before. The first shows a girl in her teens. She wears a dark dress, faintly patterned, with the voluminous sleeves of the 1870s; her hair is parted in the middle and scraped back from her face, although a few strands have escaped at the nape of her neck. Her eyes seem to be set on the middle distance and her mouth droops at the corners, as though she's looking into the past and expecting the future to be hard. In the second photo, she's in her fifties, wearing a fur collar and a hat that's decorated with an elaborate arrangement of feathers, maybe even a whole bird. Her eyes are hooded now, and her jawline shows her years, but her mouth is a tight line, and she's glaring at someone or something just outside the frame of the photo. She's glaring at her life, I tell myself.

I always knew you'd be hard on me, life. But you haven't done me in yet.

I'm drawn back to the pensive eyes of the teenaged girl, and now I play with the foolish notion that, through some power no more mysterious than the wireless channels that connect me with my distant cousin, the young Rachel looks back at a fading line of women I know nothing about, while the older Rachel looks ahead to descendents she will never know. Me, for example. And my Rachel, named for her. And now Cali.

THE CURRENTS OF CALI'S world are invisible. Cali will have no memories of a rancher grandmother who washed lamp chimneys, filled the bowls of the lamps with kerosene out of a tin container, trimmed the wicks, and struck the match that sent the shadows wavering back into the corners of the room, because Cali's grandmother touches a switch and light bursts forth. Cali won't remember her grandmother filling a pen from a small bottle of ink, won't remember the pen scratching over paper as her grandmother writes letters to her relatives, because Cali's grandmother either rattles a keyboard and touches *send* or else she taps numbers into a tiny plastic device and awakens a voice somewhere in space.

Cali knows all about the cell phone. She has a toy cell phone of her own, which she holds to her ear as she cocks her head and says, "Gobbledy-gook?" She listens for a moment. "Gobbledy-gook," she answers, and closes her phone.

NOT ALL MEMORY RESIDES in the brain, but in the hands and the arms and the pores of the skin. Because Cali has lived in my house since her birth, and because I have had so much of the care of her, I have reawakened to the liquid sound of the voice from the crib, the telltale reek of diaper, the strength in the small squirming body as she resists the diaper being changed. And I'm once again alert to the suspicious silence from this little companion of my days as, perhaps, I'm getting dressed in the morning and she's exploring the contents of my bathroom drawers.

"What have you got in your mouth?"

Cali struggles and tries to clamp her mouth shut as my probing finger extracts a hairpin or a penny or the flash of white disc that is the lid to my contact lens case.

"Oh no! Where's my contact?"

Mornings in particular are like this. I'm at the bathroom mirror, trying to make the best of my aging face, while she's on her grand adventure. She yanks open another drawer, flings out the washcloths, a package of cotton balls, nail clippers—

"Oh no! Cali, give me those before you hurt yourself!"

One of her favorite expressions is getting to be *Oh no!*

Mornings will not last forever, and afternoons will pass into evenings, and I won't always be at hand to probe her mouth and save her from the sharp and the dangerous. I think of the backward-looking eyes of the young Rachel Woodington, of that fading line of women: her mother, her grandmother, perhaps a great-grandmother stitched from shreds of stories that survived a sea crossing from distant England and then were lost.

All the lost stories. My father's childhood name for Rachel Woodington was Gobbie. Nobody knew why he called her that, but I never knew him, even in his old age, to refer to her by any name but Gobbie.

Now, as I muse on the face of the older Rachel under the brim of that bird-trimmed hat, the defiant set of her mouth and her hooded glare, I wonder if it really is the future she's trying to face down. How can Rachel Woodington, who started fires in a wood stove and cooked meals of homegrown potatoes and fried chickens she had raised and killed and butchered, who boiled water on that same wood stove and washed her grandson's clothing on a washboard and mended those clothes with her tiny, even hand-stitching, who must have read to him from the books I later found littering the floor of that upstairs bedroom that would have been freezing in winter and stifling in summer, how can Rachel Woodington possibly imagine my life of workshops and conferences and instant messaging—and, God knows, disposable diapers and bottle liners—any more than Cali can imagine a life where that bored child, her grandmother, shot her own grandmother with a homemade bow and arrow?

If I could wish for myself, if I could wish for Rachel Woodington any immortality at all, it would be to return spiderlike and shrunken to watch over the child:

No! Let me have that before you hurt yourself!

IN THE AMERICAN LIVES SERIES

To order or obtain more information on these or other University
of Nebraska Press titles, visit www.nebraskapress.unl.edu.